S0-BZK-998

40 INSTANT STUDIES

NEW TESTAMENT

TRUE TO LIFE
STORIES THAT
CHALLENGE
TEENS TO ENGAGE
CULTURE

Standard®
PUBLISHING
Bringing The Word to Life

Cincinnati, Ohio

Published by Standard Publishing, Cincinnati, Ohio
www.standardpub.com

Copyright © Standard Publishing

All rights reserved. Permission is granted to reproduce for ministry purposes only—not for resale.

All Scripture quotations are taken from the HOLY BIBLE, NEW INTERNATIONAL VERSION®. NIV®. Copyright © 1973, 1978, 1984 by International Bible Society.
Used by permission of Zondervan. All rights reserved.

Printed in: USA
Project editor: Jim Eichenberger
Cover and interior design: Symbology Creative

ISBN 978-0-7847-2299-2

15 14 13 12 11 10 09   9 8 7 6 5 4 3 2 1

CONTENTS

HOW TO USE THIS BOOK

IT'S AN AGE OF ENDLESS INFORMATION, AND STUDENTS ARE OVERWHELMED. FURTHERMORE, THEY HAVE A HARD TIME UNDERSTANDING HOW—AND EVEN *IF*—ALL THAT THEY KNOW FITS TOGETHER. THEY ARE DROWNING IN THE FLOOD OF DATA THAT POURS FORTH FROM THEIR MEDIA-RICH YET WISDOM-POOR WORLD.

Help them make a significant connection between the Bible and culture with **40 Instant Studies: New Testament**. Each two-page study is easy to prepare, yet rich with true-to-life relevance and biblical depth.

This book is designed as a resource for those in student ministry. In this volume you will find 40 easy-to-prepare lessons that can be used in a pinch or as a part of a larger strategy you have in mind. Each lesson contains:

A REAL STORY

Each lesson is contained on the front and back sides of a single sheet. Remove a lesson by tearing on the handy perforations and head to the copy machine. Make a copy of the introductory story and discussion questions for each student. Start your lesson with high student interest and involvement.

AN EASY-TO-FOLLOW LESSON PLAN

Keep the back page of the lesson to help you guide your group through a Bible study that addresses the questions raised by the introductory article. At your fingertips you have probing discussion questions and clear Scripture commentary.

A CLOSING CHALLENGE

A good Bible study should inspire one to action. At the end of each lesson is a simple activity designed to give your students something concrete to do as a result of the study. These challenges use a variety of teaching methods, but are always focused and memorable.

In addition, find a quick summary of each lesson in the table of contents. Search the Scripture index for specific Bible references used, the story index for the topics covered in the introductory activity, or the topic index to find how specific scriptural themes are handled. You will find a wealth of teaching resources at your fingertips.

In an age of information glut, you need a way to grab the attention of your students and help them apply God's Word to the world around them. Do exactly that with **40 Instant Studies: New Testament**.

Jesus Sends Out the Twelve

A Plea from the President

In order to accomplish the great task of leading a country, those in charge must talk to one another and to the citizens of that nation. Each year the president discharges that duty by making a State of the Union Address.

The State of the Union Address is an annual event in which the president of the United States reports on the status of the country, normally to a joint session of the U.S. Congress (the House of Representatives and the Senate). The address is also used to outline the president's proposals for the upcoming year.

The United States Constitution (Article II, Section 3) requires that the president make such an address:

"[The President] shall from time to time give to Congress information of the State of the Union and recommend to their Consideration such measures as he shall judge necessary and expedient." Although the Constitution does not specify details, the speech is usually given in January of each year.

For example, in January of 2007 the war in Iraq was a major issue. About two days before his State of the Union Address, President Bush announced that he would send 21,500 more U.S. troops to Iraq. Immediately most Democrats and some Republicans opposed that troop surge and built support for a nonbinding resolution opposing it. Furthermore, an opinion poll taken at that time showed that 65 percent of Americans opposed the president's handling of the war.

But in the State of the Union Address, President Bush asked Congress and the American people to give his plan a chance to work. His plea was heard. By the time the next State of the Union Address was given, the president was able to tell about the success of his once-unpopular decision.

QUESTIONS TO CONSIDER:

■ Do you usually watch the State of the Union Address each year? If not, why don't you? If so, why do you think it is important to do so? Do you think it is a good idea to require the president to make such a speech every year? Defend your answer.

■ Communication and cooperation are necessary to perform a task as great as leading a country. What do you think would happen if a leader did not communicate or if people did not cooperate with him? What other actions, attitudes, or resources are necessary to accomplish a great task? Think about the biggest job you have ever taken on. How were you prepared for it? What did you need to accomplish it?

■ Leading a country is a great task. That is why the president of the United States is required to enlist the help of fellow leaders and citizens each year with a formal speech. When Jesus called his disciples to the great task of serving him, he enlisted their help with some specific promises. Let's discover what he said.

INSTANT **STUDY** 01 ■ NEW **TESTAMENT**

Copyright © 2009 Standard Publishing. All rights reserved. Permission to photocopy for ministry purposes only—not for resale.

BIBLE TRUTHS

BIBLE**TRUTH** 1

Jesus called disciples to serve him in particular places. MATTHEW 10:5, 6

■ **What fears do you have about becoming a missionary?**

INSIDE STORY: This is the first time Jesus sent out his twelve disciples to preach and teach. He directed the disciples to the nation of Israel (v. 6). Gentiles and Samaritans (a mixed race of Jews and Gentiles) were excluded at this time (v. 5). This mission to Israel was only a first step in taking the message of the gospel to all people.

Jesus' church is described as one body with specialized parts, not a lot of bodies each trying to save the world on their own (Ephesians 4:11-13). Believers have differing missions that complement the missions of others. Paul was proud that God set him apart to "preach him among the Gentiles" (Galatians 1:15, 16). Yet Paul also recognized that God called Peter "as an apostle to the Jews." (2:8). Jesus' apostles were given specific tasks and led to particular places. The same is true of disciples today. God sends willing missionaries in which he places interest and abilities suitable for the task to which he calls them.

BIBLE**TRUTH** 2

Jesus gave his disciples needed, life-giving truth to share. MATTHEW 10:7, 8

■ **If someone were to ask you to summarize your faith in three sentences, how would you do it?**

INSIDE STORY: Note that when Jesus sent out the twelve, he did not say: "Just tell people your general impressions about me." The message to be preached was very specific: "The kingdom of heaven is near" (v. 7). Therefore anyone doing wrong should repent (Mark 6:12) because the promised Messiah of Israel had come to earth. Leaders had arisen before and claimed to be the Messiah (Acts 5:36, 37). To show that Jesus was the true Christ, the apostles

would freely share the power of the Messiah with others by performing what were unquestionably miracles from God (Matthew 10:8). Later, the Great Commission (which is still ours today) would include Christian baptism and obedience to "everything I have commanded you" (Matthew 28:20). The early church was "one in heart and mind" because of the clear and unified message of the apostles that was confirmed by the work of the Spirit (Acts 4:32).

BIBLE**TRUTH** 3

Jesus provided for the needs of his disciples as they served him. MATTHEW 10:9, 10

■ **Why is it wrong to expect something for nothing? If you get something "free," who might be paying for it?**

INSIDE STORY: Imagine that you have been hired to fry burgers at a local fast food establishment. You would expect your employer to provide you with a uniform, a nifty paper hat, the grill and grilling utensils you need, and so forth. Similarly, Jesus provided for those apostles who worked for him. They were told not to bring extra clothing or money for room and board. Those to whom they ministered by Christ's power would provide those things (vv. 9, 10). In Corinth Paul argued that he did not require the Corinthians to supply his needs, but that was his choice. Not only had other apostle used that right, but Paul also saw this as a principle of Jewish law (1 Corinthians 9:1-12). Later Paul would argue that administering elders in churches should be paid for the same reason (1 Timothy 5:17, 18). To this day, Christian missionaries travel around the world to preach the gospel and are supported by other believers. God provides for those whom he calls.

CHALLENGE

Present your students with upcoming mission opportunities available. Pray, asking God to direct your students into the paths of service he has selected especially for each of them.

Copyright © 2009 Standard Publishing. All rights reserved. Permission to photocopy for ministry purposes only—not for resale.

Feeding the 5,000

The Hamburglar

Brendall Louis Bourque has been arrested twice for the same offense. His crime? Impersonation of a police officer.

Several years ago in his hometown of St. Martinsville, a community southwest of Baton Rouge, Bourque's arrest for this crime was his first offense. Two years later, his second arrest in nearby Jennings for impersonation of a police officer was coupled with the additional charge of theft by fraud. His crime earned him the nickname, "the hamburglar."

For his second offense, the motive for Bourque's impersonation seemed to be hunger. The 34-year-old Louisiana man allegedly posed as a police officer to get free food at a local Burger King®.

Jeff Parish Detective Chris Meyers reported that Bourque entered the fast-food restaurant and presented himself to the manager as an officer of the Jennings Police Department. Bourque allegedly told that manager that the department had ordered food from the restaurant, and some of the food was missing from that order. The manager complied by giving Bourque two hamburgers, but then reported the incident to the police.

The pseudo-cop was arrested shortly thereafter and confessed to his crime. Though Bourque may have considered his deception to be a small one, the police believe his lie to have been a real Whopper®.

QUESTIONS TO CONSIDER:

■ Why do you believe it is a crime to impersonate a police officer? Why might some people commit such a crime?

■ What did Bourque see as a benefit of being a police officer? List some motives others may have for legitimately choosing a career in law enforcement.

■ List some other service-oriented jobs. What motivates people to choose each of those lines of work?

■ Brendall Louis Bourque's motive for pretending to be a police officer was obviously shallow and selfish. Yet others choose to spend their lives serving others for deeper and purer motives.

■ In Matthew 14:15-21 we read about a fast-food meal of another kind. Let's examine Jesus' motives for serving one of the most famous meals of all time.

INSTANT**STUDY 02** ■ NEW**TESTAMENT**

Copyright © 2009 Standard Publishing. All rights reserved. Permission to photocopy for ministry purposes only—not for resale.

BIBLE TRUTHS

BIBLE**TRUTH** 1

Jesus provided spiritual nourishment.

MATTHEW 14:15, 16

■ **How do you think followers of John the Baptist felt after his death? What are some ways Jesus dealt with this grief? Why do you think this would be effective?**

INSIDE STORY: Herod had just beheaded John the Baptist for the vilest of reasons (Matthew 14:1-12). Several of Jesus' disciples were once followers of John the Baptist. Jesus withdrew from the crowds and took his disciples across the Sea of Galilee to an unpopulated place (v. 13). But when Jesus got to the intended place of solitude, he found great crowds who had hurried by foot around the north end of the sea to greet him when he arrived. The crowds considered John to be a prophet (v. 5) and saw John as one who might rescue them from their suffering under Roman rule and bring in the kingdom of God.

Jesus responded by welcoming them, teaching them about the kingdom of God that they longed for, and demonstrating his authority by healing the sick among them (Matthew 14:14; Mark 6:34; Luke 9:11). When his disciples raised the practical question of feeding this group who were miles from home and the nearest inn, Jesus prepared to dramatically demonstrate that he could meet all real spiritual, emotional, and even physical needs of those in his kingdom (Matthew 14:15, 16).

BIBLE**TRUTH** 2

■ **Jesus provided physical sustenance.**

MATTHEW 14:17-19

■ **What Old Testament stories do you know that talk about food miracles? Why do you think God used this type of miracle on so many occasions?**

INSIDE STORY: God fed the Israelites in the wilderness with manna (Exodus 16:13-18). God delivered food to the prophet Elijah by using ravens (1 Kings 17:1-6). God fed a widow and her sons with a little oil that turned into gallons (2 Kings

4:1-7). Elisha fed a hundred men with twenty barley loaves (2 Kings 4:42-44). All of these deal with food, but how much greater in magnitude was the feeding of the five thousand!

Why do so many miracles in Scripture deal with food? God knows that after a very short time, our bodies cease to function without it. Therefore, these kinds of miracles show how God has the power to meet our most basic and pressing needs. Jesus took people in great spiritual and emotional need and demonstrated with this remarkable miracle that God could supply every need.

BIBLE**TRUTH** 3

Jesus provided a reminder of his power to his disciples. MATTHEW 14:20-21

■ **There were twelve baskets of leftovers and there were twelve disciples. Why would you think this was not a coincidence?**

INSIDE STORY: Why the twelve baskets of leftovers? The word for basket in these verses refers to a small pouch that a person would wear around his waist. Perhaps the disciples each had a lunch basket of leftovers to carry with them to remind them of this event. Jesus would later use those leftovers to contrast the power of his teaching to the empty legalism of the current religious establishment (Matthew 16:5-9).

God gives reminders of his greatest miracles. The rainbow was given to remind us of his grace after the flood (Genesis 9:16). The Jews were told to tie tassels on the ends of their garments to remind them that they were literally covered by God from head to foot (Numbers 15:39, 40). Most importantly, Christians have been given the feast of the Lord's Supper to regularly remember God's greatest work in the death, burial, and resurrection of Jesus (1 Corinthians 11:24, 25).

CHALLENGE Suggest that the next time your students go to a restaurant with their friends they order only a beverage rather than food, then donate what they would have spent on that meal to an organization that feeds the hungry in Jesus' name.

Copyright © 2009 Standard Publishing. All rights reserved. Permission to photocopy for ministry purposes only—not for resale.

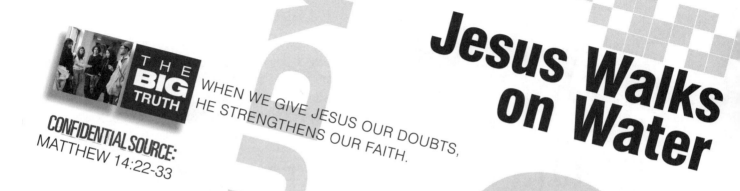

THE BIG TRUTH

CONFIDENTIAL SOURCE:
MATTHEW 14:22-33

WHEN WE GIVE JESUS OUR DOUBTS, HE STRENGTHENS OUR FAITH.

Jesus Walks on Water

Prom Therapy

Most high schools across the country hold a spring prom each year. Around that same time, the Memorial Sloan-Kettering Cancer Center (MSKCC) puts on their own version of prom, a dance for all ages of pediatric patients, from high schoolers down to toddlers.

MSKCC started the annual event more than fifteen years ago. It was a simple gathering for a handful of children well enough to head to the playroom. Now the dance has grown to about eighty participants. Patients can choose from donated formal gowns and tuxes to wear on the big day. The hospital cafeteria is transformed into a dance hall, complete with decorations and a DJ. Volunteers help dancers get ready, painting faces for the younger kids, painting fingernails for the girls, and finding hats for the boys.

Shannon Callagy (age sixteen) said, "When you don't really feel that well, you don't see anyone. But this is nice. We can all have fun here together."

Natalia Harris (age twelve) said, "I want to dance around because I can't—I've danced all my life, but I can't dance now."

Some dancers remained attached to their IV poles, but it didn't stop the fun. Family and friends, as well as doctors and nurses joined in the party.

Erin Chance has a five-year-old son, Patrick, at the hospital. She said, "This means a lot. He definitely associates the hospital with a lot of pain. His treatment is very painful and it makes him feel very bad, so to see him here and having fun with his friends, his nurses, it's great. To see him out there, healthy, energetic, and just moving around means the world."

Some patients begin to socially withdraw during long and painful stays at the hospital. Dr. Farid Boulad noted what a good experience the prom is for the patients: "On that day, everything that has to do with cancer is gone. And they are the kings and queens and they're beautiful."

QUESTIONS
TO CONSIDER:

■ Have you ever been treated for cancer or do you know someone who has? How did the experience make you or the other person feel, both physically and emotionally? What benefits do you think the hospital prom has on the patients who attend?

■ In the article, we read that some patients withdraw while going through cancer treatments. Imagine how students your age feel when dealing with cancer and isolation in a hospital. They probably feel unsure of themselves at times. Discuss a time when you felt unsure of yourself.

■ MSKCC is trying to encourage its young patients with the prom and other events so that the students feel more sure of themselves. In a similar way, Jesus provided reassurance to His disciples when they felt unsure and experienced times of doubt. Let's read about one of those experiences now.

Copyright © 2009 Standard Publishing. All rights reserved. Permission to photocopy for ministry purposes only—not for resale.

BIBLE TRUTHS

BIBLE**TRUTH** 1

Jesus responds to doubt by calming our fears.
MATTHEW 14:22-27

■ **List some of your fears. What ideas or attitudes lie behind many of our fears?**

INSIDE STORY: After Jesus fed the five thousand, the people wanted to make Jesus king (John 6:14, 15). To avoid the mob, Jesus sent his disciples ahead of him across the Sea of Galilee while he prayed on a lonely mountainside (Matthew 14:22, 23). In the middle of the night (3:00 to 6:00 AM), Jesus finished praying and walked across the sea to catch up with his disciples (vv. 24-26). They were about three and a half miles shore at this point (John 6:19). Across the darkened waves the disciples saw a figure walking on the water, and they were terrified. Jesus' response was to immediately calm their fears (Matthew 14:27).

God's call to courage is a virtual refrain throughout Scripture. He called on Joshua to be courageous (Joshua 1:6), Elisha's servant not to fear (2 Kings 6:15-17), and even Mary the mother of Jesus not to be afraid (Luke 1:26-33). He tells the very same thing to us today when trouble strikes.

BIBLE**TRUTH** 2

Jesus responds to doubt by inviting us to take risks. MATTHEW 14:28, 29

■ **What does it mean to step out of your comfort zone? Tell about a time when you did just that.**

INSIDE STORY: In the midst of the disciples' confusion, Jesus identified himself. Such a remarkable event surely added to the disciples' confusion. Peter blurted out an offer to join Jesus on the water (v. 28). So Jesus said, "Come" (v. 29). That single word encouraged Peter to climb over the side and walk on the surface of the sea.

Throughout biblical history God has revealed his will to his servants. As was the case with Peter, that revelation raised as many questions as it answered. So God consistently took the next step. He invited his servant to "go for a test drive." God appeared to Moses in the burning bush and challenged him to confront Pharaoh (Exodus 3:1-12). Likewise, God called Jeremiah to step out of his comfort zone and into God's service (Jeremiah 1:1-10). Even today God often responds to our doubts by encouraging us to take risks.

BIBLE**TRUTH** 3

Jesus responds to doubt by supporting us when we fail. MATTHEW 14:30, 31

■ **Tell about a time when someone gave you a second chance. How did you respond?**

INSIDE STORY: When Peter took his focus off Jesus, he became afraid and began to sink. Jesus reached down and pulled Peter out of the water. Jesus asked Peter, "Why did you doubt?" (vv. 30, 31). This was certainly a rhetorical question, for who wouldn't doubt that it was possible to stay on top of the stormy surface!

It is not unusual for those whom God calls to have setbacks. When that happens, God steadies his servant and gives him or her strength to continue. David betrayed the trust of God and his nation by seducing Bathsheba and having her husband killed. But God spared his failed servant's life. David did suffer the loss of an infant son and the betrayal of a grown son later on because of his crimes (2 Samuel 12:7-14). But God did not leave him. King Manasseh was even more corrupt, leading Judah into unspeakable sin. As a result, God allowed the king of Assyria to capture and imprison Manasseh. Yet because Manasseh was willing to turn from his sin, God restored this king to power (2 Chronicles 33:9-13).

CHALLENGE

To close, play "Name that Tune." Give students a line from a hymn or worship chorus with the word trust or faith in it and have them guess the title. Discuss what each song says about trusting Jesus in the storms of life.

Copyright © 2009 Standard Publishing. All rights reserved. Permission to photocopy for ministry purposes only—not for resale.

CONFIDENTIAL SOURCE:
MATTHEW 20:1-16

GOD'S GRACE GOES FAR BEYOND ANYTHING WE CAN FIND IN THIS WORLD.

The Workers in the Vineyard

Book Worm

Fans of J. K. Rowling just couldn't wait until *Harry Potter and the Deathly Hallows* went on sale. But this impatience made many of them victims of an offer that came with some very malicious strings attached.

A few weeks before the seventh book in the Harry Potter series went on sale, an e-mail appeared in many an inbox promising a sneak preview of it. The offer of a free book nearly a month before it hit the shelves may have seemed too good to be true. *It was!*

Although the attachment to the message appeared to be a Microsoft Word file, it was something much more sinister. The file was actually the W32/Hairy-A worm, a computer virus. Allysa Myers, a researcher with McAfee Avert Labs said the worm "doesn't try to steal any system information . . . it just makes system changes such that your system becomes largely unusable."

The virus had several "payloads," or tasks it performed. It created a text file that read, "Harry Potter is a dumb kid; so is Daniel. Ron Weasley is ugly but who cares? Hermione is pretty and exploited but who cares? Dumbledore is old and haggard but who cares? JK Rowling was an ex-witch but who cares, betcha didn't know. All we care is that . . . Harry Potter is gonna die! Okay, you can now get yourself a copy of the dumb Harry Potter book."

Furthermore, the worm searched for detachable drives to infect, causing the user to innocently plant the virus in other computers. In addition, an infected computer would display a message every time it was turned on, calling for the user to repent. Additional user accounts for the computer were created for the book's main characters, and many of the computer's system tools including the clock and the firewall were isabled. Also, when connecting to the Internet, the computer automatically went to a page selling a book making fun of the Harry Potter series. In short, one small file would take over the entire computer.

"This is an 'old school' virus, written to give the author a platform to show off rather than to steal identities or cash," said Graham Cluley, senior technology consultant for the Internet security firm called Sophos. "This person isn't being driven by the desire to inflate his or her bank account but by a loathing for J. K. Rowling and her incredibly popular books."

QUESTIONS TO CONSIDER:

■ Have you ever had any experience with a computer virus? How were you tricked into allowing it to be installed on your computer? What did it promise? What were the negative consequences?

■ What are some other ways people are deceived by promises that have strings attached? How does being tricked in this way change people's attitudes about trusting others?

■ Many appealing offers in life have strings attached! But the saying, "If it seems too good to be true, it probably is" does not apply to God. God has made many wonderful promises to those who believe in him. Today we will see that God's offer of grace is available to all—no strings attached!

Copyright © 2009 Standard Publishing. All rights reserved. Permission to photocopy for ministry purposes only—not for resale.

BIBLE TRUTHS

BIBLE**TRUTH** 1

God's grace is not a limited time offer.
MATTHEW 20:1-7

■ **How do advertisers use limited time offers to lure customers? How does God's promise of salvation differ from these kinds of offers?**

INSIDE STORY: Limited time offers are meant to appeal to a shopper's pocketbook. Buy now and save money! Pick one up today or lose out! But limited time offers only last so long.

God's grace is not limited. It is fully extended to all who wish it. The offer lasts throughout this age. This is the first point Christ made in this story. Even as the workday drew almost to an end, the workers were sought out and found by the landowner.

Peter may have recalled this parable years later when battling false teachers who mocked the belief in the second coming. Peter answered the reason the age did not end immediately was because of God's patient desire that all come to repentance (2 Peter 3:9).

God's incessant grace is available when we are ready. No one is born too soon or too late. Early comers don't have an advantage over those who are born thousands of years after Jesus first offered God's grace.

BIBLE**TRUTH** 2

God's grace will not be used up. MATTHEW 20:8, 9

■ **Consider the experience of shopping on Christmas Eve or being near the end of the buffet line at a large reception. How did that experience differ from the experience of those who were last to come to work in this parable?**

INSIDE STORY: Those who came to work for the landowner later in the day did not receive "leftover" wages. They received a full day's wage. The Apostle Paul saw himself as one who came to work in God's vineyard later in the day. After listing hundreds of people who saw the resurrected

Christ, Paul listed himself. He was busy chasing righteousness through law keeping when Jesus called his first disciples. He even persecuted those disciples. His birth into the kingdom was like "one abnormally born," but he still received full benefits of God's grace (1 Corinthians 15:5-8). Paul described himself as "the worst of sinners," but he still received God's "unlimited patience" (1 Timothy 1:15, 16). There is reward in Heaven of course, but grace itself is given in full dose and does not run out before it reaches the last person to enter the kingdom of God.

BIBLE**TRUTH** 3

God's grace does not exclude the unlovely.
MATTHEW 20:2, 10-16

■ **Why might people in this parable still be seeking jobs later in the day? Who might be these "late arrivers" in the church today?**

INSIDE STORY: Perhaps the late-risers had problems that made them undesirable employees. But the landowner hired them and gave them equal standing with the others. This was a troubling message to the early church. Many feared that allowing pagan Gentiles to become Christians would lower the moral standards of the church. Therefore, some taught that Gentiles who converted must first keep the law of Moses (Acts 15:1, 5). Peter and James the brother of Jesus refused to say that law keeping earned any part of salvation (Acts 15:7-19).

This message of inclusiveness still troubles many in the church today. But the job of the Christ's church is to redeem the broken, not simply to accept those who already meet our expectations.

CHALLENGE
Help students take a moment to think of a person they know who needs God's grace. Have them write that name on a small scrap of paper and pray for opportunities to reach out with God's acceptance to that person.

INSTANT**STUDY** 04 ...CONTINUED

Copyright © 2009 Standard Publishing. All rights reserved. Permission to photocopy for ministry purposes only—not for resale.

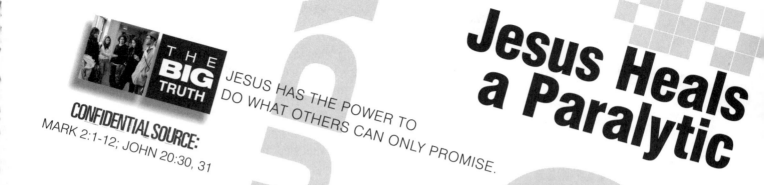

Jesus Heals a Paralytic

Unbelievable Beasts

Here are two remarkable stories from the animal world.

Perky lives—A few years ago, a hunter shot a ring-neck duck and took it home. He put it in the refrigerator before he prepared the bird for the dinner table. Two days later, the hunter's wife opened the refrigerator door and was surprised when the should-have-been-dead duck raised its head and looked back at her.

The woman called her daughter, and both of them took the duck to a local veterinarian. After treating the duck's broken wing, the vet sent it to the Goose Creek Wildlife Sanctuary in Tallahassee, Florida.

"Everybody's been calling her the *Lucky Duck*, but tonight one of my volunteers called and said they want to name her *Perky*, because she really has gotten so much better," said Noni Beck, wildlife rehabilitator at the wildlife sanctuary.

A few days later, Perky stopped breathing during a surgery to repair some of her gunshot damage. Veterinarian David Hale revived the bird after several tense moments by performing CPR. "I started crying, 'She's alive!'" Beck said after the incredible duck cheated death a second time.

Cujo returns—Cujo, a frisky seven-year-old golden retriever, sneaked out of the Barczewski family's yard in St. Louis several years ago. Six and a half years later, thinner and grayer and with a history of remarkable coincidences behind him, the dog returned to the Barczewski family.

After slipping away, Cujo ended up in Columbia, Missouri, 120 miles from home. An elderly woman adopted the dog and renamed him *Willy*. When that woman entered a nursing home, the dog went to another nursing home to be a pet for the residents there. But Cujo/Willy was too active to be confined indoors, so he was put up for adoption. His picture was posted on the Web site of a golden retriever rescue group.

Shortly thereafter, a relative of the Barczewskis was looking at the Web site, hoping to adopt a dog of his own. He immediately recognized the dog and arranged to have him reunited with his original family. "It's a miracle," exclaimed forty-one-year-old Noreen Barczewski. "We found him!"

QUESTIONS TO CONSIDER:

■ Sometimes stories are hard to believe. What do you find hard to believe about the animal stories that you have just read? Mrs. Barczewski called her pet's story "a miracle." Do you agree with that description of events? Why or why not?

■ Tell about something that you would find hard to believe had it not happened to you. What aspects of your story might seem hard to believe to someone else, even though you know they are true? Would you call your experience "a miracle"? Why or why not?

■ We may call an unlikely event "a miracle." Yet a true miracle is more than just a group of stunning coincidences or unlikely occurrences. The Bible tells us that Jesus performed real miracles—he used his supernatural power to overrule the processes of this natural world. Let's look at what Jesus accomplished by performing miracles.

Copyright © 2009 Standard Publishing. All rights reserved. Permission to photocopy for ministry purposes only—not for resale.

BIBLE TRUTHS

BIBLE**TRUTH** 1

Jesus' miracles drew seekers to him. MARK 2:1-4

■ **What would cause you to travel for miles to see someone you have never met? Why did people travel so far to see Jesus?**

INSIDE STORY: In Capernaum, a large crowd of people followed Jesus to the home where he was staying (vv. 1, 2). At that place Jesus "preached the word to them" (v. 2). The expression "the word" is used to describe early Christian preaching and teaching (Acts 6:4; Galatians 6:6). What caused such a crowd to gather? Mark tells us that Jesus' reputation had already "spread quickly over the whole region of Galilee" after he had driven an evil spirit out of a man (Mark 1:27, 28). After healing a leper a while later, Jesus was so in demand that he could no longer "enter a town openly" (v. 45). Jesus' miracles drew crowds.

In the crowd that day was a group of men who brought a paralyzed friend to Jesus for healing (Mark 2:3). The size of the crowd prevented them from entering the house in a conventional manner, so they improvised by lowering their friend through the dried mud and grass-thatched roof (v. 4). Even though they had little knowledge about Jesus' teachings, his reputation for miracles probably stirred their faith and longing for the promised Messiah that would cause "the lame [to] leap like a deer" (Isaiah 35:6).

BIBLE**TRUTH** 2

Jesus' miracle caused seekers to think about what was truly important. MARK 2:5-11

■ **Would you be more impressed with someone who claimed to heal disease or with someone who claimed to be able to make people right with God? What might be some problems with your type of thinking?**

INSIDE STORY: Jesus said to the paralytic, "Son, your sins are forgiven" (v. 5). Jesus' statement brought a silent but critical reaction from the teachers of the law (vv. 6, 7). They

understood that only God could forgive sin (2 Samuel 12:13; Psalm 32:1-5; Isaiah 43:25). They were appalled that Jesus was claiming to be God. Such blasphemy was punishable by death (Leviticus 24:16).

Jesus responded with two questions: "Why are you thinking these things?" (Mark 2:8) and "Which is easier: to say to the paralytic, 'Your sins are forgiven,' or to say, 'Get up, take your mat and walk'?" (v. 9). The first forced the religious leaders to consider Jesus' divinity shown by his ability to know their thoughts. The second allowed the entire crowd to think about what was truly important. Physical suffering is a symptom of the separation from God caused by sin. While the former demands our attention, it is the latter—reconciliation with God—that we truly need.

BIBLE**TRUTH** 3

Jesus' miracles left no doubt as to the truth of his teaching. MARK 2:12; JOHN 20:30, 31

■ **How would you define "blind" faith? How does blind faith differ from what Jesus requires of us?**

INSIDE STORY: Jesus told the paralytic, "Get up, take your mat and go home" (v. 11). The man responded in faith and "walked out in full view of them all" (v. 12). No one could deny what had happened. No one could refute Jesus' testimony. The crowd responded in amazement and praise. John explains why Jesus' miracles are recorded in Scripture: "These are written that you may believe that Jesus is the Christ, the Son of God, and that by believing you may have life in his name" (John 20:30, 31). Jesus' miracles established his deity and confirmed his message. None of the Gospel writers recorded all of Jesus' miraculous deeds (John 21:25), but those we know about are certainly adequate, along with the rest of God's Word, to lead us to faith.

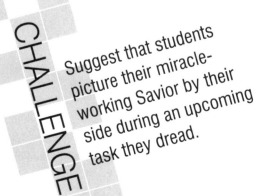

CHALLENGE

Suggest that students picture their miracle-working Savior by their side during an upcoming task they dread.

Copyright © 2009 Standard Publishing. All rights reserved. Permission to photocopy for ministry purposes only—not for resale.

Jesus Calms the Storm

Stormy School Year

Some things can be scheduled. Some cannot. While the graduation ceremonies for McDowell County schools were scheduled a year in advance, no one could foresee how the year would end for students of these schools.

Several years ago, floods devastated this county in West Virginia in early May. The McDowell County Board of Education was forced to cancel classes for the remainder of the school year. Damage to the area was estimated at $16 million. Roadways were severely damaged, and more than 2,000 county homes and businesses were damaged or destroyed. All eighteen McDowell County schools were damaged, and one was completely destroyed. By mid-June, however, the three high schools of McDowell County held their commencement ceremonies, despite the seemingly long odds of doing so.

Superintendent Dr. Mark A. Manchin stated that it was the goal of the board, however, to try to hold the graduations at Big Creek, Iaeger, and Mount View High Schools as scheduled. "We didn't want school to end with students' last memory of the floods," agreed Mount View Principal Barbara Hairston.

David W. Falin of the MCNA Bank in Welch gave the commencement address at Mount View High. Falin expressed the sentiments of many residents of the county by telling graduating seniors, "Life has already thrown you a lot of curves."

QUESTIONS TO CONSIDER:

■ What other examples of the unpredictability of nature can you name?

■ Have you every felt that, in the words of Mr. Falin, "Life has already thrown you a lot of curves"? Explain.

■ How does knowing that our lives are too complex for anyone to control fully make you feel?

■ McDowell County could plan graduation ceremonies far in advance, but they could not foresee the floods that almost cancelled them. We live in a very unpredictable world, and there is little we can do about it!

■ In Mark 4:35-41 the disciples of Jesus experienced the power and unpredictability of nature's storms. This Bible story reveals three truths that will help us as we face storms in our lives.

Copyright © 2009 Standard Publishing. All rights reserved. Permission to photocopy for ministry purposes only—not for resale.

BIBLE**TRUTH** 1

Even when we are with Jesus, storms will come.
MARK 4:35-37

■ **Agree or disagree: Being a Christian means I will have a trouble-free life. Defend your answer.**

INSIDE STORY: Jesus and his disciples began to cross over to the eastern side of the Sea of Galilee (Mark 4:35). This area was heavily Gentile territory, probably a scary destination for the disciples. Furthermore, Jesus went "just as he was" (v. 36), at the end of a busy day for both him and the disciples.

Suddenly, without warning, the boat was caught in a furious storm. It wouldn't be hard to imagine the feelings of the disciples at this point. They had seen Jesus show compassion upon those he barely knew—healing incurable diseases and casting out pernicious demons. Surely his closest disciples could expect equal or better care! But there they were—being dragged toward the unknown dangers of Gentile territory, exhausted from their daily routine, and now hanging on to their boat for dear life while he was nowhere to be found. Didn't they deserve better than this?

Christians are sometimes surprised when they encounter the figurative storms of life. If God loves us, shouldn't we be immune to life's heartaches? As was the case with the disciples, having Jesus in the boat does not mean that storms will not come.

BIBLE**TRUTH** 2

Storms may cause even those closest to Jesus to question his love. MARK 4:38

■ **What has happened to you that made you wonder if God really loved you?**

INSIDE STORY: We don't know how long the disciples fought the storm before they tried to rouse Jesus. Finally, they woke him, shouting above the sound of the storm, "Teacher, don't you care if we drown?" Theirs was the call of

desperation and fear mixed with frustration and doubt. This cry was not an unusual one throughout biblical history. A quick survey of the Psalms will reveal opening lines such as, "Answer me when I call to you, O my righteous God" (4:1); "Why, O Lord do you stand far off?" (10:1); and "How long, O Lord? Will you forget me forever?" (13:1), to name but a few. When tough times come, we may question his love. But as was the case with these first disciples, storms are not evidence of God's rejection of his children.

BIBLE**TRUTH** 3

Surviving storms with Jesus' power will strengthen even the weakest faith. MARK 4:39-41

■ **Atheist philosopher Friedrich Nietzsche wrote, "What does not kill me, makes me stronger." Why do you agree or disagree? After Jesus calmed the storm, how might have the disciples paraphrased this quote?**

INSIDE STORY: Jesus rose and said, "Quiet! Be still!" (Mark 4:39). Suddenly, the wind died away and the sea calmed down. Then Jesus turned to them, saying, "Why are you so afraid? Do you still have no faith?" (v. 40). If they had been fearful of the storm, it was nothing compared to their fear when the storm calmed. "Who is this?" they stammered. "Even the wind and waves obey him!" (v. 41).

The disciples received a clearer picture of their Lord and Savior by enduring this storm with him. Adversity is a good teacher for Christians today as well. By riding out one of life's storms with Jesus, we can grow in our faith, gaining new insight about the one who came to save us. Christians need not "be surprised at the painful trial[s]" we suffer "as though something strange were happening" (1 Peter 4:12). When the storms of life come, we can be sure that Jesus is still in our boat!

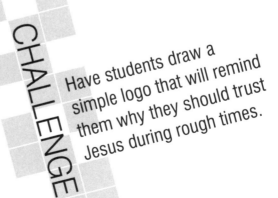

CHALLENGE

Have students draw a simple logo that will remind them why they should trust Jesus during rough times.

INSTANT**STUDY** 06 ... CONTINUED

18

Copyright © 2009 Standard Publishing. All rights reserved. Permission to photocopy for ministry purposes only—not for resale.

Jesus Restores a Girl's Life

A Cancer Clue

A few years ago, British scientists thought that they may have discovered a clue that will help them stop one of the deadliest forms of skin cancer. The science journal *Nature* reported that the Cancer Genome Project, based at Hinxton, Cambridgeshire, identified a gene that may be responsible for malignant melanomas.

Two years before scientists at the Wellcome Trust Sanger Institute in Hinxton began a search for cancer genes existing among the estimated 30,000 human genes. The team worked by looking for differences between the DNA in cancerous cells and that of normal cells.

They found that a gene involved in controlling cell growth was mutated in about 70 percent of those with malignant melanomas, a deadly form of skin cancer. In the United Kingdom, 6,000 new cases of malignant melanoma are diagnosed each year and 1,700 people die from the disease. In the United States, 54,000 new cases are reported each year, and 7,400 people die from it.

"This discovery," affirmed Dr. Andy Futreal, of the Wellcome Trust's Cancer Genome Project, "opens up a window that we hope to explore for potentially developing a new therapeutic drug."

"The most exciting thing about this discovery," added Professor Mike Stratton, also of the Cancer Genome Project, "is that it could be a direct lead to new treatments for malignant melanoma. According to Stratton, it would take about five years to identify a save treatment and several more years to thoroughly test it. He estimates that a drug to treat this deadly disease could be available in fifteen years.

Yet, even Stratton is cautious about guaranteeing the success of this project. "Cancers are devious beasts," he warns. "They are unpredictable, and they do not always respond in the way we would like them to."

QUESTIONS TO CONSIDER:

■ Why do you believe this news caused excitement in the medical community? Why is a lot of time and money invested in the treatment of cancer? Has cancer affected your family in any way?

■ Other than seeking cures for deadly diseases, what are some other ways people attempt to postpone death?

■ How would you react to someone who claimed to have discovered how you could live forever?

■ This story about a skin cancer cure is certainly good news. Yet despite this breakthrough and others like it, we still doubt that we will ever be able to prevent death completely. We will always have to struggle with the reality of our mortality.

■ In Mark 5:21-43 we read the story of Jairus, a man who had to deal with the reality of death to someone very close to him. Let's discover three attitudes and actions present in Jairus when he faced the death of his daughter.

19

Copyright © 2009 Standard Publishing. All rights reserved. Permission to photocopy for ministry purposes only—not for resale.

BIBLE TRUTHS

BIBLE**TRUTH** 1

People seek Jesus when illness strikes home.
MARK 5:21-24

■ **Referring to those under fire in battle, it is said, "There are no atheists in the foxholes." What does that mean to you? How does that idea apply to Jairus in these verses?**

INSIDE STORY: A man of high standing, Jairus was responsible for the conduct of the assemblies for public worship. Among the things he did, he appointed those who would read Scripture, lead in prayer, and preach. Knowing his position, we wonder how difficult it might have been for him to seek out Jesus for assistance to his only daughter (Luke 8:42). But it was with urgency that he fell at the feet of Jesus and pleaded with him to come and put his hands on his daughter so that she might be healed and live.

Perhaps Jairus understood the mistake of King Asa from the history of his nation. When this king was afflicted with a deadly disease, "he did not seek help from the LORD, but only from the physicians" (2 Chronicles 16:12). When the reality of our mortality strikes home, we need to leave our comfort zones and humbly seek the great physician.

BIBLE**TRUTH** 2

People react to death with fear and doubt.
MARK 5:35, 36

■ **Has death ever taken a loved one from you? How did you feel? How do you think Jairus felt in this story?**

INSIDE STORY: Media mogul Ted Turner is an outspoken critic of Christianity. A sibling of his died as a child. A God that would not save the life of a child, he reasons, is a God worthy of his contempt. Note that Jairus also had his doubts and fears. As he and Jesus were on their way to his daughter, word came to them that the child was dead. How crushed Jairus must have been by the news. But Jesus merely said, "Don't be afraid; just believe" (v. 36).

The apostle John may have been recalling this incident years later when he wrote, "There is no fear in love. But perfect love drives out fear, because fear has to do with punishment. The one who fears is not made perfect in love" (1 John 4:18). Jairus began to doubt God's love and power, causing him to fear a terrible God who would take the life of an innocent child. Jesus reassured him that God was not that way and proceeded to demonstrate that fact in a remarkable manner.

BIBLE**TRUTH** 3

Obedience to God in the face of death is the only response that makes sense. MARK 5:37-43

■ **How has the threat of ridicule caused you to change your behavior? How did Jairus react in the face of ridicule?**

INSIDE STORY: Jesus confronted the mourners at Jairus' house by saying, "The child is not dead but asleep" (v. 39). There is no question that the young girl had actually died, for there were many people to attest to that fact. As they laughed at him, Jesus saw to it that the mourners were put out of the house. Then he went to the twelve-year-old girl, took her by the hand, and said, "Little girl, I say to you, get up!" (v. 41). She immediately stood up and walked among them. Jesus told her astonished parents to give her something to eat, further evidence that life had returned.

Ridicule is a strangely powerful type of argument. It would have been tempting for Jairus, hearing the jeers of his friends, to join with them and drive Jesus away from his home. Job's own wife encouraged him to reject a belief in God when disaster struck their family (Job 2:9). When believers suffer, it is tempting to yield to those ridiculing our faith and refuse to remain loyal to God. Jairus, however, withstood such temptation and received the reward of his faith.

CHALLENGE Ask students to write inscriptions for their own tombstones that would reflect faith in Jesus to conquer death.

Copyright © 2009 Standard Publishing. All rights reserved. Permission to photocopy for ministry purposes only—not for resale.

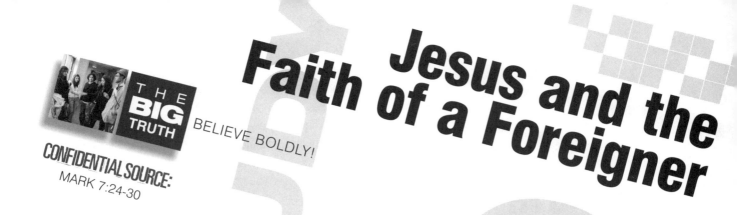

THE BIG TRUTH — BELIEVE BOLDLY!

CONFIDENTIAL SOURCE:
MARK 7:24-30

Jesus and the Faith of a Foreigner

Faithful Friends

The Boy Scout camping trip turned into a nightmare for the family and friends of eleven-year-old Brennan Hawkins. Brennan had gone with a friend to the Bear River Boy Scout Reservation in the High Uintas Wilderness, about eighty miles east of Salt Lake City, Utah. Shortly after Brennan enjoyed the climbing wall, which wasn't that far from the main camp, he must have wandered off. An hour later, Scout leaders worried when Brennan didn't show up for dinner.

Fortunately, the story has a happy ending. Four days later, a volunteer searching for Brennan found him five miles west of where he was last seen. "I turned a corner and there was a kid standing in the middle of the trail. He was all muddy and wet," said rescuer Forrest Nunley. "He was a little delirious. I sat him down and gave him a little food."

Around 3,000 people joined the search for Brennan at first, but after a few days only about 350 people were still looking. What's interesting is that Nunley started off in a different direction than the rest of the search team. Sheriff Dave Edmunds had predicted that Brennan would have gone down the valley along the river. "Typically children walk downhill, along the least path of resistance," he said. So the majority of the searching was down in the river area. But Brennan had climbed about 600 feet higher, up into the mountains. That's where Nunley, who drove up the mountain on his ATV, found him.

Brennan had no food or water with him, and his family said he did not have a good sense of direction. What helped Brennan was that the night temperature had been mild, only in the mid fifties, and the weather had been good. "I think you have to thank the Lord," said another volunteer, Deon Evans. "The second Brennan was in the ambulance, the heavens opened up and it began to rain."

The area is only fifteen miles from where another Scout, Garrett Bardsley, disappeared a year before. Sadly, Garrett's story did not end as happily as Brennan's; Garrett was never found. "When we came off this mountain in the winter, my friends and I decided right then, if anyone came missing, we'd be there immediately," said Garrett's father, Kevin Bardsley, who joined in the search for Brennan. "I never stop thinking about my son, and I never will the rest of my life."

QUESTIONS TO CONSIDER:

■ Have you ever needed help searching for someone or something that was lost? Who did you ask to help you search? Did others volunteer to help you? Did you find what you were looking for?

■ Brennan Hawkins's parents had to place their trust in complete strangers as they searched for their son. Do you easily trust people? Why or why not? What types of people do you generally have a hard time trusting?

■ If we have a hard time trusting other people, how easily will we trust God? Jesus' disciples wanted to trust God, but the same time, they were raised to distrust people who weren't Jewish. During the final year of Jesus' ministry, he took a trip outside of Israel to give his disciples an unlikely illustration of faith. Let's examine that story.

Copyright © 2009 Standard Publishing. All rights reserved. Permission to photocopy for ministry purposes only—not for resale.

BIBLE TRUTHS

BIBLETRUTH 1

Faith acts with urgency. MARK 7:24, 25

■ **Where is the first place we turn when we are in need? What did the woman in this Bible story do?**

INSIDE STORY: To get away from the crowds, Jesus traveled from Capernaum to Phoenicia, a journey of about forty miles. This is one of only two times the Bible mentions that Jesus journeyed into a foreign country. The other was his journey with his parents into Egypt when he was a baby.

In Phoenicia Jesus met a woman whose daughter was possessed by a demon. She was a Gentile, a woman of Canaanite ancestry (Matthew 15:22). Her faith in Jesus was first illustrated by her urgency. Wasting no time, she "came and fell at his feet" without delay—"as soon as she heard about him" (Mark 7:25). Have we ever said, "I guess we just need to pray about it," treating divine intervention as a last resort rather than our first hope? This woman's rush to Jesus' feet is a powerful picture of faith.

BIBLETRUTH 2

Faith overcomes cultural prejudices. MARK 7:26

■ **What kinds of people make you uncomfortable? Why might this woman feel uncomfortable around the disciples? Why might they not have wanted to be around her?**

INSIDE STORY: The people in Syrophoenicia were generally worshipers of Ashtoreth and Baal. Note that this woman did not rush to her native religion but to this visiting Jewish teacher. What faith it took to reject her cultural conditioning and seek help from beyond the norms of her society!

Cultural prejudices run both ways. Jesus' disciples were annoyed with her. She seems to have made her emotional requests not only in the house but also on the road outside. Jesus first met her entreaties with silence (Matthew 15:23). Nevertheless, she did not give up. The disciples asked Jesus to send her away. Yet the faith of this woman pressed her to seek God even when she felt uncomfortable.

BIBLETRUTH 3

Faith is not sabotaged by ego. MARK 7:27-30

■ **What attitudes are being expressed when someone says, "I don't take charity!"? What contrasting attitudes did the woman in this story express?**

INSIDE STORY: The grace of God may present an obstacle to the proud who believe that they have virtues that should earn their salvation. Note how Jesus used this situation to illustrate grace to his disciples. When this woman presented her request, Jesus responded, "It is not right to take the children's bread and toss it to their dogs" (v. 27), pointing out that she was in no position to ask him for anything. She was not even Jewish!

It would have been easy for the woman to storm off muttering in indignation. Nevertheless, she *was* asking for something that she did not deserve. So she replied, "But even the dogs under the table eat the children's crumbs" (v. 28). She acknowledged her unworthiness as well as the fact that even an unearned crumb from the hand of God was more valuable than the most lavish of feasts obtained anywhere else.

CHALLENGE Ask students to memorize 2 Peter 1:5-8 this week and pray that God add one of the virtues Peter mentions to their faith.

Copyright © 2009 Standard Publishing. All rights reserved. Permission to photocopy for ministry purposes only—not for resale.

THE BIG TRUTH

CONFIDENTIAL SOURCE:
MARK 8:22-26

JESUS IS ALWAYS AT WORK IN OUR LIVES,
CHANGING US ONE STEP AT A TIME.

Jesus Heals a Blind Man

Courting Constitutionality

For six years, Kentucky county officials took steps to try to legally display the Ten Commandments in a public place. In the end, they did not succeed.

A little history of the Kentucky case, *McCreary County v. ACLU*, is helpful. In 1999, a framed copy of the Ten Commandments was put on display in the McCreary County courthouse. This display resulted in a lawsuit saying that displaying the Ten Commandments violated the separation of church and state.

In the next stage of the conflict, McCreary County officials tried to add to the display in order to make it legal. Next to the framed copy of the Ten Commandments, officials added other documents about the role of religion in American history. These included the national motto of "In God We Trust" and a copy of the Congressional Record declaring 1983 the "Year of the Bible." These changes did not appease the opposition, however.

As a final step, officials made the display even larger. Other documents including the Bill of Rights, the Mayflower Compact, and framed lyrics of "The Star-Spangled Banner" were added, making the display a large collage of historical documents.

The Supreme Court was not impressed. The Court agreed with a lower court that called the modified display a "sham" that tried to hide the religious intent behind it. The majority of justices believed that McCreary County was not sincerely trying to be neutral toward religion.

It is probable that these decisions are not the last words the Supreme Court will have on the subject of public religious displays. After all, the Supreme Court building itself has a carving that illustrates Moses receiving the Ten Commandments! Nevertheless, it is still not completely clear what steps local governments must take to make such displays legal.

QUESTIONS TO CONSIDER:

■ What steps did the officials of McCreary County take to display the Ten Commandments? If you were in their positions, would you have taken different actions at any stage of this process? If so, what?

■ In our country, trials often proceed in stages. Decisions of local courts can be appealed to district courts and finally to the U.S. Supreme Court. Give some other examples of actions that are taken in stages, one step at a time.

■ Justice seems to be an ongoing process. In our lives, God's work in us is also an ongoing process, accomplished one step at a time. Today we'll read how Jesus worked in stages to change the life of a man who was blind.

INSTANT**STUDY 09** ■ NEW**TESTAMENT**

Copyright © 2009 Standard Publishing. All rights reserved. Permission to photocopy for ministry purposes only—not for resale.

BIBLE TRUTHS

BIBLE**TRUTH** 1

Those seeking Jesus must be prepared to leave their comfort zones. MARK 8:22, 23A

■ **What did Jesus require of the blind man? Why do you think he might have made that request?**

INSIDE STORY: Before healing him, Jesus took the blind man by the hand and led him out of the village.

In the Old Testament, the messenger of God often required a simple act of obedience before a miracle took place. The people of Israel were commanded to march around Jericho (Joshua 6:3-5). Elijah asked the widow of Zarephath to bake him a small cake (1 Kings 17:13-16). Elisha ordered Naaman to bathe in the Jordan River (2 Kings 5:10). These acts were simply token acts that demonstrated the trust of the seeker.

In this case, Jesus asked the blind man to go with him outside of the city limits. Perhaps Jesus was seeking to build a relationship with the man. Perhaps he was seeking a quiet place to perform a miracle. Ultimately, Jesus was asking a blind man to leave familiar surroundings, go to an undisclosed location, and place himself totally in Jesus' care.

BIBLE**TRUTH** 2

The immature in Christ must continue to seek vision from him. MARK 8:23B-25

■ **What about this miracle is different from other healings of Jesus? What might have been Jesus' purpose?**

INSIDE STORY: This is the only recorded miracle of Jesus that seems to be gradual. The man's sight came in stages. In all of the other miracles, the healing seems to be instantaneous. This reminds us not to be impatient when Jesus does not bring about the changes we desire for our lives as quickly and as dramatically as we desire.

Doctors today often prescribe antibiotics to cure infections. Typically, the symptoms disappear after a few days of treatment. Nevertheless, the patient is warned to continue the treatment until all the medicine is gone. All too often,

patients discontinue taking the medication only to find the infection returning. Although all of us who accept Jesus as Savior have overcome sin and death, we must continue the treatment. We must seek his victory over this world daily until that day in which our salvation is complete.

BIBLE**TRUTH** 3

Mature Christians must obey his voice over their own agendas. MARK 8:26

■ **Note that Jesus gave one positive and one negative command after the healing. Think of other times God commands us to do one thing and not do another. What does that say about Jesus' being our Lord?**

INSIDE STORY: Jesus told the man to go home, but not to go through the village. It must have been exciting for him to be able to walk *alone*, without the usual helpful arm to lean on. The man's friends may have gone to his home to wait for what would happen. If they were there and watching for him, they must have burst into joyous celebration when they saw him coming down the street alone!

This healing from Jesus came with a command that required a certain follow-up action (go home) but forbade another (don't go into the village). A leper who was healed was commanded to testify to the priest but not to tell anyone else (Mark 1:44). The Gadarene demoniac was told to go home to testify to his family about his healing but was not allowed to go with Jesus and his disciples (Mark 5:18, 19). Jairus and his wife were told to minister to the hunger of their resurrected daughter but not to go tell everyone about the miracle (Mark 5:43). The overriding issue is clear: the lordship of Christ. If Jesus has the authority to heal, he also has the authority to command. When the Lord is at work in our lives, it is not up to us to call the shots. We must obey his voice over our personal agendas.

CHALLENGE

Paul would later write, "He who began a good work in you will carry it on to completion until the day of Christ Jesus" (Philippians 1:6). Students should think of something Jesus has begun to do in their lives and pray daily that he will make them aware of how he wants to complete that work in them.

Copyright © 2009 Standard Publishing. All rights reserved. Permission to photocopy for ministry purposes only—not for resale.

Jesus Heals Blind Bartimaeus

JESUS OFFERS MERCY TO ALL WHO COME TO HIM.

CONFIDENTIAL SOURCE:
MARK 10:46-52

It's a Cruel World

Sometimes the world is an angry, scary place. These stories tell of some of the ways people can hurt others in both big and small ways.

Now cut that out!—Eighteen-year-old Naydiet Magang claimed that she was doing nothing more than walking down the streets of Des Moines, Iowa. Magang told police officers that another teen came up behind her and began cutting her hair. In trying to get the scissors, Magang says she was cut on the hands and face. The other girl disputed this account, saying that it was Magang who had the scissors and began giving *her* the unwanted haircut.

Police are still sorting out the conflicting claims. While Magang did have cuts on her hands and face, the alleged suspect was missing "a large quadrant of hair from the front of her head," according to official police reports. Crime scene investigators were called to take photographs of injuries and haircuts.

Kidnapping, family style—The sister of a Brazilian soccer star, Ricardo Oliveira, was kidnapped from her home. Two hooded gunmen broke into the home of Maria de Lourdes Silva de Oliveira in Sao Paulo, overpowering her husband and children. Police suspect that her fourteen-year-old son, who had allegedly threatened to kidnap his mother on other occasions, was involved in the crime.

In another strange kidnapping case, a woman from Seville, Spain, is accused of faking the kidnapping of her fifteen-year-old son in order to extort over one million dollars from her estranged husband. The teen is accused of calling his father on the telephone and begging him to pay the ransom. The mother and son were allegedly successful with this scheme three times before the father became suspicious and hired a private investigator.

Just like Romeo and Juliet—In an incident reminiscent of a Shakespearean tragedy, a Pakistani man committed suicide outside his fiancée's home after he thought he accidentally killed her. Ahmed Ashraf was shooting a gun in the air outside his fiancée's home as part of his efforts to persuade her to get married two months early when a stray bullet accidentally hit her. The young woman fell down screaming, "I have been shot." Thinking he killed her, Ashraf shot himself. The young woman's injuries were minor, and she survived.

QUESTIONS TO CONSIDER:

■ Choose one or more of the news stories mentioned above. How would you feel if you were the victim in this case? How easy would it be for you to forgive the people involved? Explain.

■ Tell about a time when you felt like a victim. How does it feel when you think that even those closest to you don't really care about you?

■ We all want someone in our lives to care about us. Sometimes it seems that we are the victims of a cruel, heartless world. Today we will look at a man who may have felt that way before Jesus came into his life. Let's see how Bartimaeus sought and reacted to the mercy offered by the Savior.

Copyright © 2009 Standard Publishing. All rights reserved. Permission to photocopy for ministry purposes only—not for resale.

BIBLE TRUTHS

BIBLE**TRUTH** 1

Approach Jesus boldly. MARK 10:46-48

■ **Tell about a time you needed help but were afraid to ask. Contrast that with the actions of Bartimaeus.**

INSIDE STORY: When Jesus and his disciples were leaving the city of Jericho, a large crowd was following. But this did not faze Bartimaeus; he cried out to Jesus for help. Those around him cautioned that he was making a fool of himself, but this blind man was convinced that Jesus could and would help him (Mark 10:46-48).

Bartimaeus heard the names "Jesus" and "Messiah." From others he heard about miracles Jesus had worked— especially the recent raising of Lazarus from the dead (John 11:38-44; 12:17-19). By using the term "Son of David," Bartimaeus was confessing that he believed that Jesus was the promised Christ (Matthew 22:41, 42). He also knew that the prophets promised that the Messiah would be sent to "proclaim freedom for the prisoners and recovery of sight for the blind" (Isaiah 61:1, 2; Luke 4:18, 19). He was also confident that the Christ would "sympathize with our weaknesses" and would hear the cry of one who would "approach the throne of grace with confidence" (Hebrews 4:14-16).

Bartimaeus shows us how to turn to God when we are in need. We come to him believing "that he exists and that he rewards those who earnestly seek him" (Hebrews 11:6). Do you need something from God? "You do not have, because you do not ask God" (James 4:2).

BIBLE**TRUTH** 2

Describe your need clearly. MARK 10:49-51

■ **Imagine yourself in the doctor's office. He asks you what is wrong. How would you respond? Compare that with how Bartimaeus responded to Jesus.**

INSIDE STORY: True, the great physician "knows what you need before you ask him" (Matthew 6:8) and the Spirit can discern the meanings behind our most unintelligible grunts

and groans (Romans 8:26, 27). Nevertheless, we are expected to do our best to clearly communicate to God. We need to knock at God's door and tell him what we need, knowing that he will answer in a way that is best for us. A loving father would certainly be expected to act in our best interests (Matthew 7:7-11). We do not need to remain anxious about our needs but should "present [our] requests to God" (Philippians 4:4-7). Getting what we need does have some relationship to asking and asking with proper motives (James 4:2, 3).

Jesus asked Bartimaeus a simple question. The blind man gave a lucid response: "Rabbi, I want to see" (Mark 10:51). When we come to God for help, we need to know what we want. Bartimaeus certainly did.

BIBLE**TRUTH** 3

Follow Jesus gratefully. MARK 10:52

■ **Remember wanting a certain toy as a child? What did you promise your parents if they bought it? Did you keep your promise? Notice how Bartimaeus responded after his request was granted.**

INSIDE STORY: Bartimaeus received his sight. The trust shown by going to Jesus and believing he was who he claimed to be healed him. In response, Bartimaeus "followed Jesus along the road" (Mark 10:52).

Those who received mercy from Jesus responded with grateful allegiance. Peter's mother-in-law responded with service (Mark 1:29-31). The Gadarene demoniac wanted to follow Jesus but obeyed when Jesus sent him back to his family (5:18-20).

CHALLENGE

Close the session with your students praying with outstretched hands, approaching God for mercy, and clearly telling God what they need. Imagine Jesus responding to those pleas and your students responding to him. What would they say to him?

Copyright © 2009 Standard Publishing. All rights reserved. Permission to photocopy for ministry purposes only—not for resale.

The Sower, the Seed, and the Soil

THE BIG TRUTH

CONFIDENTIAL SOURCE:
LUKE 8:4-15

AFTER THE SEED OF CHRIST IS PLANTED, IT NEEDS TO GROW.

Ever-changing Change

A Greek philosopher named Heraclitus (540 BC-480 BC) said it well: "Nothing endures but change." These stories seem to confirm the philosopher's musings.

Memory chipped—Pocket calculators, cell phones, handheld computers, and other electronic devices have made life easier. But they may have also affected our ability to think for ourselves. "People have more to remember these days and they are relying on technology more for their memory," said Ian Robertson, professor of psychology at Trinity College, Dublin.

A recent survey revealed that a quarter of those polled said they couldn't remember their home phone number, while two-thirds couldn't recall the birthdays of more than three friends or family members. Two-thirds of those who responded said that they relied on their phone or electronic organizer to remember important information for them. Those who grew up with all of these devices remembered far less information than those over fifty years old who recall life without personal electronics.

The fifty-year-old teenager—Recently, toy-maker Mattel Incorporated has garnered growing profits. The growth was not because of any fantastic new product. On the contrary, it was the result of increased sales of the fifty-year-old Barbie doll. In the 1950s, most dolls looked like infants, but Ruth Handler noticed that her daughter Barbara often enjoyed giving her dolls adult roles. Despite the initial resistance, Handler was able to convince Mattel to create a doll that resembled an adult more than a baby. Barbie, "Teen-age Fashion Model," was featured at the American International Toy Fair in New York on March 9, 1959, and changed the toy industry. Now more than fifty years later, Barbie is still making a huge difference in the company's profits.

QUESTIONS TO CONSIDER:

■ What do you think are the most significant changes in the world during your lifetime? If you could make one change in the world right now, what would it be? What person or group of people do you think has been most successful in making important changes in the world?

■ Let's bring this discussion to a personal level. Name some things in your own life you would like to change. What would it take for those changes to come about?

■ We all see a need for change, but whether at the worldwide level or the personal level, positive changes do not come easily. In one of his most famous parables, Jesus taught about three things that keep positive change from happening.

Copyright © 2009 Standard Publishing. All rights reserved. Permission to photocopy for ministry purposes only—not for resale.

BIBLE TRUTHS

BIBLE**TRUTH** 1

We cannot grow if we harden our lives to God's Word. LUKE 8:5, 11, 12

■ **When have you stubbornly resisted authority? What happened? What does Jesus say happens when we resist the authority of God's Word?**

INSIDE STORY: In Jesus' day, a farmer would plant by scattering a handful of seed across his field. Naturally, this method sent some of the seed to the wrong places. Some seed fell on the path, where it was trampled by people and eaten by birds (v. 5). The seed in this parable represents God's Word. When it fell on hard and unresponsive people, the devil soon took away the seed, and they did not believe (vv. 11, 12).

We also see other examples of this stubborn resistance in Scripture. Pharaoh saw the power of God but did not submit to it (Exodus 4:21). When the kings in the northern areas of Canaan saw God miraculously giving victory to the people of God, they still resisted God's army (Joshua 11:20). Zedekiah saw the words of God spoken by Jeremiah fulfilled but still rejected them (2 Chronicles 36:11-13).

On May 10, 1977, actress Joan Crawford lay on her deathbed. When her housekeeper began to pray aloud for her, Crawford reportedly cursed and warned the woman, "Don't you dare ask God to help me."

BIBLE**TRUTH** 2

We cannot grow if we do not let God's Word penetrate the depths of our lives. LUKE 8:6, 13

■ **What does it mean when we say a person is shallow? What happens to someone with a shallow faith?**

INSIDE STORY: Some of the farmer's seed fell on the surface bedrock, where it sprouted and soon withered. The thin layer of soil over the rock did not have room for the deep roots that were necessary to sustain the plant.

In the early days of the church, Philip preached in Samaria. A local magician named Simon was emotionally moved by the awesome miracles God performed by Philip. Simon, like many other Samaritans, believed and was baptized (Acts 8:9-13). Apparently, however, the Word of God did not penetrate to the depths of Simon's life and crowd out his old life as a magician. When Peter and John arrived, Simon actually tried to buy from them the right to empower others with the Holy Spirit (vv. 18, 19)! Peter diagnosed Simon's shallow faith saying, "For I see that you are full of bitterness and captive to sin" (v. 23).

In 1977, pornographer Larry Flynt briefly converted to Christianity. Flynt, however, never allowed his faith to develop roots and quickly renounced Christianity.

BIBLE**TRUTH** 3

We cannot grow if we let lesser pursuits crowd the Word of God from our lives. LUKE 8:7, 14

■ **Pastor Bill Hybels wrote a book called *Too Busy Not to Pray*. Looking at the story of the thorny ground, what do you think that title means?**

INSIDE STORY: More of the seed fell into patches of thorns. The young plant grew, but was soon overpowered by the weeds surrounding it and was choked out. Jesus identified these weeds as "life's worries, riches and pleasures" (v. 14). A young faith will compete with the everyday concerns of life. John talked about these concerns competing with God for the friendship of the follower of Christ (1 John 2:15, 16).

Judas saw the same miracles and heard the same teachings as the rest of Jesus' twelve disciples. Also, Judas had the special responsibility of caring for the finances of Jesus and his disciples (John 13:29). We also learn that he embezzled from those funds (John 12:6). Could it be that the worries and riches associated with Judas's duties were weeds that strangled his faith?

CHALLENGE Say this to the students: "Imagine yourself in an unfamiliar room and that you are wearing a blindfold. Think about how you feel. If that unfamiliar room represents the future God has for you, what particular sin of yours might that blindfold represent? What can you do to take off your blindfold this week?"

INSTANT **STUDY** 11 ... CONTINUED

Copyright © 2009 Standard Publishing. All rights reserved. Permission to photocopy for ministry purposes only—not for resale.

THE BIG TRUTH

CONFIDENTIAL SOURCE:
LUKE 9:57-62

WHEN WE DECIDE TO FOLLOW JESUS,
LIFE WILL NEVER BE THE SAME AGAIN.

Jesus Calls for Commitment

Anti-Valentine's Day

In recent years, unmarried women outnumber married women in our country. While this fact may seem insignificant to some, it has meant huge profits for some creative marketers. They have turned Valentine's Day into Anti-Valentine's Day.

Clever businesses have found many ways to turn loneliness and bitterness into big bucks. For those who are not in a romantic relationship, "a lot of it is, 'I'm going to refuse to sit here and wallow,'" said Ellen Garbarino, a marketing professor at Case Western Reserve University.

The Corner Alley, a bowling alley and nightclub in downtown Cleveland, hosted a "Love . . . Spare Me!" party featuring nonromantic music and "love stinks" specials on their menu. Matt Brick, Web host of www.antivday.com, has sold thousands of "I think, therefore I'm single" T-shirts and bumper stickers. Twinsburg High School in Ohio held an Edgar Allan Poe Festival for an Anti-Valentine's Day event, featuring a reading of the anything-but-romantic "The Tell-Tale Heart." Old Town Lansing (Michigan) threw a party in which participants could go on a "stupid cupid" scavenger hunt for black hearts and shred pictures of their exes.

American Greetings Corporation of Cleveland offered an entire line of Anti-Valentine's cards aimed at single women. Some sample cards read:

I promise, you won't be alone forever . . .
I know how much you like cats.
Valentine's Day: When Hades and holidays collide.
It's Valentine's Day, so here's a card with a heart inside . . .
I'd tell you whose it is, but the less you know, the better.

"For everyone, Valentine's Day isn't just about hearts and roses," said Alana Campana, Valentine's Day program manager at the card company. "It's really an unmet market."

QUESTIONS TO CONSIDER:

■ Have you seen Anti-Valentine's Day cards this year or heard of Anti-Valentine's events in your community? What do you think of them? How did the growing number of single people in the country help spark this phenomenon? Why could that population shift be called a turning point?

■ Think of some other turning points in human history. How did those changes help determine events that followed them?

■ Whether we have a "special someone" or not, Christians have chosen to begin a love relationship with Jesus. That decision to walk in obedience to him is a crucial turning point in life. Let's look at the changes that come after that important turning point.

Copyright © 2009 Standard Publishing. All rights reserved. Permission to photocopy for ministry purposes only—not for resale.

BIBLE TRUTHS

BIBLE**TRUTH** 1

Are you willing to live with less? LUKE 9:57, 58

■ **List things you are not willing to live without. Do we trust the one we follow to provide for us? Explain.**

INSIDE STORY: On one occasion, Jesus tested the commitment of men who thought they were ready to be his followers. The first man was an eager volunteer, ready to follow Jesus anywhere. But was he willing to have less than even an animal—to have no place to lay his head? (Luke 9:57, 58).

Jesus made a similar challenge to one that we often call the rich young ruler. This man implied that he was willing to do anything to gain eternal life (Mark 10:17). When Jesus told him that he needed to stop counting on his material wealth and follow him instead, the man was saddened and left (vv. 21, 22). Jesus concluded the lesson to his disciples by promising that material goods given up to follow him would not be missed either in this age or the next (vv. 28-31). Those of us who follow Jesus today also need to recognize that we must not let possessions be more important to us than our Savior.

BIBLE**TRUTH** 2

Are you willing to examine your life's purpose? LUKE 9:59, 60

■ **Describe who you are. What difference would it make to your description if you defined yourself first and foremost as a follower of Jesus?**

INSIDE STORY: A second man was ready to follow Jesus right after he buried his father (Luke 9:59). His father had not yet died, but it was customary in that day for a child to live close to his parents until the parents were dead and buried. The man was saying that he would be free to follow Jesus at that time. Jesus insisted, however, that following him had to be the most urgent priority of all. In other words, this man was being called to a higher purpose than simply being a good son.

Jesus used similar words when first sending his twelve disciples out to minister for the first time. Anyone who put a higher priority on family (as important as family is) than on following Jesus was not worthy of following him (Matthew 10:34-39). This is true of any purpose in life. Being a father is a beautiful and godly position, but unless one is a Christian first, a father cannot accomplish the purpose for which he was created. The same is true for being a teacher or a doctor or a cook or a member of any other line of work. A *job* is not the same as a *calling*. Only Jesus provides the latter.

BIBLE**TRUTH** 3

Are you willing to establish new relationships?
LUKE 9:61, 62

■ **Whom do you know that is living in the past? Why shouldn't a Christian live in the past?**

INSIDE STORY: A third man wanted first to go back home and say farewell to his family. He wanted to reserve the right to value his past without Jesus as highly as his future with him (v. 61). Jesus used a farming image to respond. To plow straight furrows the farmer would keep his eyes fixed on a point ahead of him. Looking back would ensure that these furrows would be crooked (v. 62). If he were speaking today, Jesus might compare such a person to one who looked behind him while driving a car to see where he had been.

No doubt Jesus' audience thought of Lot's wife when Jesus used the words "looks back." Lot's wife was called out of her old life in Sodom by God but still wanted to hold on to it. As a result, she got her wish by becoming a permanent part of the landscape (Genesis 19:15-17, 26). In the New Testament, James described this attitude as "friendship with the world" (James 4:4). Jesus wants his disciples to look to the new relationships he has in store for them in the future rather than live a life pining for the "good old days!"

CHALLENGE Challenge students to create an acrostic poem using the word commitment. Each line of the poem should begin with a letter in that word and be a word or phrase describing something that could prevent or discourage someone from keeping a commitment to Jesus.

Copyright © 2009 Standard Publishing. All rights reserved. Permission to photocopy for ministry purposes only—not for resale.

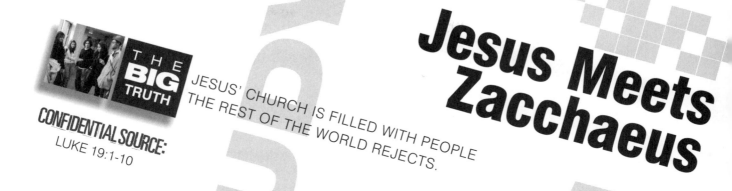

THE BIG TRUTH

CONFIDENTIAL SOURCE:
LUKE 19:1-10

JESUS' CHURCH IS FILLED WITH PEOPLE THE REST OF THE WORLD REJECTS.

Jesus Meets Zacchaeus

Unlikely Disciples

What kind of teens and young adults do you expect to follow Jesus? Lauren Sandler researched that topic and found surprising results. Sandler is a former reporter for National Public Radio and a self-described "secular Jew." She reports her findings about what she calls "the disciple generation" in her book—*Righteous: Dispatches from the Evangelical Youth Movement.*

In Iowa, Sandler interviewed leaders from Extreme Tour Events, an organization that uses rock music and extreme sports to reach "at-risk" youth with festival-style events. Sandler witnessed a half-pipe show in which those believers reached out to skaters. The group attempts to build relationships with youth who are ignored or shunned by many local congregations.

In Seattle, the birthplace of the grunge music scene a couple of decades ago, the reporter attended the Mars Hill Church. That mushrooming megachurch reaches tattooed musicians and other members of the arts community with a countercultural message that is culturally liberal yet theologically conservative.

On the other extreme of unchurched teens are the future lawyers and politicians of our country. Sandler visited those reaching out to that group of young people at Patrick Henry College in Virginia. According to the college Web site, "The mission of Patrick Henry College is to prepare Christian men and women who will lead our nation and shape our culture with timeless biblical values and fidelity to the spirit of the American founding."

Sandler was surprised when she met the son of former PTL evangelists Jim and Tammy Faye Bakker. Members of Jay Bakker's Revolution Church in New York City sit "on folding chairs and bar stools, juggling cocktails and cigarettes," reports Sandler. She also discovered that Ryan Dobson, the son of Focus on the Family's founder James Dobson, rides a motorcycle and sports tattoos but claims to believe the same things as his father. "As far as my dad and I see it, we look different and talk different, but that's it."

Ms. Sandler's book is very critical of all of these efforts, since she rejects the message of Jesus. Yet she seemed genuinely touched when one group of young people she visited took time to pray for her and her relationship with the Savior they follow.

QUESTIONS TO CONSIDER:

■ List some of the types of people in this article who seem unlikely to follow Jesus. (Don't forget the author of the book!) In your opinion, why do people believe that these individuals are not interested in becoming Christians?

■ Name some other groups of people that seem unlikely to follow Jesus. What characteristics do you picture a disciple of Jesus having? How might those ideas affect your efforts at evangelism?

■ Unlike many, Jesus places no boundaries dictating what types of people can follow him. Let's see what happened when Jesus called an unlikely candidate, by his society's standards, to be his disciple.

Copyright © 2009 Standard Publishing. All rights reserved. Permission to photocopy for ministry purposes only—not for resale.

BIBLE**TRUTH** 1

Zacchaeus left his questionable practices when called by Jesus. LUKE 19:8

■ **What was so bad about being a tax collector in Jesus' day? What happened when Zacchaeus followed Jesus?**

INSIDE STORY: Tax collectors were highly paid yet detested. Typically, the government required a fixed amount of revenue from an assigned territory. Whatever the collector could gather above that amount (by any means necessary) was his to keep. Furthermore, tax collectors were also considered traitors, since taxes supported the occupying Roman army. Jews who would take money from their brothers and give it to their captors were certainly worthy of contempt! Despite this, Jesus paused during his trip through Jericho, commanded that Zacchaeus come down from his vantage point in a tree, and invited himself to the tax collector's house (Luke 19:5, 6). As did the disciple Matthew when Jesus called him to abandon his tax collection booth, Zacchaeus responded with repentance (Matthew 9:9). In a show of that repentance, Zacchaeus pledged half of his wealth to the poor and promised to make the restitution required by Jewish law for fraud (Luke 19:8).

BIBLE**TRUTH** 2

Jesus can bring the worst of sinners into his kingdom. LUKE 19:1, 2, 9, 10

■ **What is the most questionable occupation you can think of? How would you expect a person in such a job to change were he or she to become a Christian?**

INSIDE STORY: Zacchaeus had learned to work the corrupt system well. He had risen to the level of "chief tax collector" (Luke 19:2), which meant that he had not only engaged in an immoral occupation, but also made it a career and mentored others in this questionable work. He was *not* a nice man! Understanding this makes Jesus' pronouncement of Zacchaeus' salvation even more shocking (v. 9). Imagine

the reaction! Even the most corrupt individual was redeemable. In fact, seeking those kinds of people and bringing them back to the road that leads to God was the very reason Jesus came to earth (v. 10).

Even today notorious sinners seek Jesus. Politician Charles Colson sought to follow Christ after being involved in the Watergate scandal. One time gang leader Nicky Cruz has tried to convince other gang members to follow Christ after he began doing so nearly fifty years ago. Former stripper Amy Dupree quit that degrading job and began a ministry dedicated to call other women out of the sex industry and to Jesus.

BIBLE**TRUTH** 3

Some people feel threatened by the grace offered to others. LUKE 19:7

■ **Think of the worst sinner you can think of. How would you react if that person claimed to become a follower of Christ? How did people react when Zacchaeus followed Christ?**

INSIDE STORY: When Jesus called Zacchaeus, the crowd criticized Jesus for associating with people they considered unworthy (Luke 19:7). The same thing happened when Jesus called Matthew to be his disciple (Matthew 9:11). When they should have been rejoicing, the crowd had nothing to offer but condemnation.

Grace is threatening to those who use religion to control others. When Paul and Barnabas brought the gospel to the mission field, they were opposed by some who taught that converts needed to prove themselves good enough by being circumcised and following the law of Moses before being accepted by the church (Acts 15:5). Such attitudes are still reported today because some churches are reaching out to skater punks, people with substance abuse problems, and other so-called "undesirables." How tragic.

CHALLENGE

Brainstorm a list of words to describe non-Christians. Make another list of words Jesus would use to describe the same people. Brainstorm ways to start making those lists more alike.

Copyright © 2009 Standard Publishing. All rights reserved. Permission to photocopy for ministry purposes only—not for resale.

Jesus and the Thief on the Cross

Difficult Forgiveness

In January 1956, five missionaries were speared to death as they tried reaching out and ministering to the Waodani tribe in Ecuador. Despite their grief, several family members of the murdered men eventually went back to the Waodani tribe and found an opportunity for friendship. The once extremely violent tribe was overcome by God's love shown in the missionaries' lives and in the Bible, and the Waodani way of life was changed. This story that has touched countless lives over the years was told in a dramatic film titled *End of the Spear.*

A large part of *End of the Spear* depicts the Waodani point of view. Anthropologists once described the Waodani as "the most violent people in human history." The movie tries to portray the tribe's fears of outsiders and rival tribes that led to so much killing and then how drastically their lives changed once they heard about God. Mincaye, a tribe member who is depicted in the movie, said, "We acted badly, badly until they brought us God's carvings [the Bible] . . . and now we walk His trail."

Mincaye's story is what inspired Mart Green, producer of the film, to want to make *End of the Spear.* Mart heard Mincaye speak the words above at a conference in 1997. At that conference, Mincaye stood side by side with Steve Saint, son of one of the murdered missionaries, Nate Saint. Steve ended up living among the Waodani, and his children today even call Mincaye "Grandpa." Yet Mincaye was one of the men who murdered Nate Saint and the other missionaries.

Once Mart witnessed firsthand the power of God, forgiveness, and unconditional love seen in Steve and the other missionary family members, he hoped their story would someday be told in film. He just didn't expect to be the one to see it through. But what was placed in his heart wouldn't go away. So Mart sought out Steve Saint to get permission to make a movie. Steve had been approached by other filmmakers in the past but said he saw something different in Green's request. So he said yes, but then said that Mart would need to ask the Waodani's permission before proceeding with the movie. After all, it was their story too.

So in 1999 Mart traveled with Steve to Ecuador, seeking permission from the Waodani to make *End of the Spear.* They quickly said no. Apparently, they had been misrepresented by other media outlets in the past and did not want it to happen again. But then Steve told the tribe members about the school shooting at Columbine that had just occurred and other violence in the United States. That got their attention. Mart said that the tribe members changed their minds. "Oh, that's just like we used to act, killing for no reason," the Waodani said. "If our story can help North America, then you tell our story."

QUESTIONS TO CONSIDER:

■ How do you think the family members of the murdered missionaries found the strength to forgive the Waodani? Do you think you could forgive such an act and then minister to the murderers? Explain. How do you think the Waodani tribe members felt once they realized the guilt of their actions? How do you think their story could help life in the United States today?

■ Do you find it hard to forgive people who murder? Explain. What other types of crime do you find it hard to believe that God would forgive? Name a time when someone hurt you and you found it hard to forgive that person.

■ It's hard to forgive people who have hurt us. It's easier to hold a grudge and be unkind to them. Jesus has a very different style. Let's take a look at a time Jesus forgave a man convicted of capital punishment.

Copyright © 2009 Standard Publishing. All rights reserved. Permission to photocopy for ministry purposes only—not for resale.

BIBLE TRUTHS

BIBLE**TRUTH** 1

The thief on the cross was a criminal found guilty of a capital crime. LUKE 23:32

■ **Why was this thief guilty of a capital crime? How are we like him?**

INSIDE STORY: Both of the criminals crucified next to Jesus were guilty of the crime of robbery (Mark 15:27). The Greek word used tells us that these thieves were not sneak thieves who break in and steal during the night (Matthew 6:20; 24:43). The men crucified with Jesus were plunderers *(lestai)* who took innocent lives in the course of their criminal activity. The death penalty was certainly deserved by these desperate criminals.

Although we may not be criminals, James makes it clear that our sin carries a death sentence with it. "Each one is tempted . . . by his own evil desire. . . . and sin, when it is full-grown, gives birth to death" (James 1:14, 15). No man sins cheaply. The penalty for sin is eternal death—separation from God. Like the thieves on the crosses next to Jesus, we are guilty of capital offenses.

BIBLE**TRUTH** 2

The thief on the cross saw the contrast between his moral nature and that of Jesus. LUKE 23:39-41

■ **What contrast did this man make between himself and Jesus? Why is that difference important?**

INSIDE STORY: While his partner mocked Jesus, the other thief would not (v. 41). This condemned criminal certainly saw the difference between his moral nature and that of Jesus as he hung beside him. Elsewhere in Scripture we see a clear contrast between Jesus and the rest of us—condemned sinners each and every one. While "we all, like sheep, have gone astray," Jesus "did not open his mouth" in his own defense when "he was crushed for our iniquities" (Isaiah 53:5-7). Jesus, "who had no sin," took

the death penalty for all sinners (2 Corinthians 5:14, 15, 21). He suffered an undeserved death so that we may have undeserved eternal life (1 Peter 2:22-25).

The thief on the cross did not deny or attempt to rationalize the guilt he knew he had. Denying guilt does not make it go away. We need to recognize that we have fallen short of the standard Jesus himself set for us.

BIBLE**TRUTH** 3

The thief on the cross knew that Jesus could grant him access to the kingdom of Heaven. LUKE 23:42, 43

■ **How did this thief respond to what he knew about himself and Jesus? How should we respond?**

INSIDE STORY: This humble thief sought Jesus' mercy and forgiveness as he suffered through his punishment alongside his Savior. Jesus assured this criminal that he would join him that very day in paradise, indicating that his sins had been forgiven. This message given to the thief becomes the message of the remainder of church history—"Everyone who calls on the name of the Lord will be saved" (Acts 2:21). On the day of Pentecost Peter commanded, "Repent and be baptized, every one of you, in the name of Jesus Christ for the forgiveness of your sins. And you will receive the gift of the Holy Spirit" (Acts 2:38). Paul repeated the same promise to Roman Christians (Romans 10:13), encouraging them to "confess with your mouth, 'Jesus is Lord,' and believe in your heart that God raised him from the dead" (v. 9). Those who "call on the name of our Lord Jesus Christ," as did the thief on the cross, will be placed among the community of the redeemed (1 Corinthians 1:2).

CHALLENGE In the hymn "It Is Well with My Soul," Horatio G. Spafford wrote: "My sin, oh, the bliss of this glorious thought!/My sin, not in part but the whole/Is nailed to the cross, and I bear it no more/Praise the Lord, praise the Lord, O my soul!" Meditate on these words with your group.

INSTANT**STUDY** 14 . . . CONTINUED

Copyright © 2009 Standard Publishing. All rights reserved. Permission to photocopy for ministry purposes only—not for resale.

Ten Lepers Ask for Help

Grateful Nominee

A few years ago, Gene Luen Yang was in for a pleasant surprise. A work of his became the first graphic novel (a.k.a. comic book) to be nominated for a National Book Award.

Yang, a high school computer science teacher, wrote and illustrated *American Born Chinese*. He was gratified when the National Book Foundation nominated the book for an award in the Young People's Literature category. Yang's main character in the comics is a young man who is struggling to figure out how to fit into his surroundings where he is the only Chinese-American in his school.

Yang says that he drew from his own experiences to create this character. "I wore glasses and I was really skinny, and I knew that I was stereotyped as a nerd," says Yang. In fact, Yang's insecurity in his identity as well as his desire to fit in caused him to put away his drawing supplies for a while. In junior high, a friend saw Yang's comics and said, "That's so geeky, why are you doing that?" Yang stopped drawing for a while but picked it back up in college.

Yang is glad to see that Asian American students today are more comfortable with their heritage. "I see the difference in my students and how I was. They're much more aware of Asian culture. And they're much more proud. They wear their skin with a comfort that I didn't have."

Yang was surprised that *American Born Chinese* was nominated for a National Book Award. He was surprised that his publisher had submitted his book to be considered in the first place. "I can't say it's a dream come true," Yang wrote on his publisher's Web site, "because it never even would have occurred to me to dream it. It wasn't in my reality. I was speechless."

American Born Chinese did not end up winning the award. Nevertheless, the nomination alone was a significant breakthrough for the graphic novel.

QUESTIONS TO CONSIDER:

■ Consider Yang's quote after hearing that his graphic novel had been nominated: "I can't say it's a dream come true because it never even would have occurred to me to dream it. It wasn't in my reality. I was speechless." Based on this quote, how would you imagine that Yang might react if *American Born Chinese* had won the award (boastful, humble, etc.)? Whom do you think he would thank in his acceptance speech?

■ If you won an award, how would you react? If you had to give a thank you speech for that award, whom would you thank? How would people react if a person received a great honor but then refused to offer thanks?

■ It is appropriate to say thanks for rewards and recognition. But how do we say thanks for an undeserved gift motivated by the love of the giver? We can learn a lot about acceptance speeches from a leper who thanked Jesus.

Copyright © 2009 Standard Publishing. All rights reserved. Permission to photocopy for ministry purposes only—not for resale.

BIBLE TRUTHS

BIBLE**TRUTH** 1

The leper made showing gratitude his first priority. LUKE 17:11-15

■ **Why do you think most of the lepers did not return to give thanks? Tell about a time when you let your excitement about a gift overshadow the need to give thanks.**

INSIDE STORY: When receiving a treasured gift, the giver is sometimes forgotten. As Jesus was heading toward Jerusalem, ten lepers called out to him from a distance (Luke 17:11-13). The law of Moses required them to be quarantined outside of a village and warn anyone who approached of their condition (Leviticus 13:45, 46). Jesus promised these men the gift they had only dreamed of. He commanded them to go into town and have a priest examine them for the purpose of declaring them cured (Luke 17:14, Leviticus 14:1-8). On their way, they looked down and saw the signs of disease fading from their bodies. No doubt they ran even faster! One of the ten, however, did not follow his emotions. He ran back to thank the one who gave this precious gift of healing (Luke 17:15). The others made using their new gift their first priority. This one leper made gratitude his first priority.

BIBLE**TRUTH** 2

The leper thanked Jesus personally. LUKE 17:16

■ **How did the leper say thanks to Jesus? How can we show that attitude when we thank someone today?**

INSIDE STORY: The one leper who thanked Jesus knew that showing gratitude requires personal investment and shows respect. He ran back and "threw himself at Jesus' feet" (Luke 17:16). This was the ultimate show of respect and humility in biblical times. Abigail knelt before David when approaching him with a peace offering (1 Samuel 25:24). Queen Esther knelt before King Xerxes after Haman's plot had been exposed (Esther 8:3). Synagogue leader Jairus knelt before Jesus when asking him to heal his daughter (Mark 5:22, 23). The leper knew how to say thanks with respect. Today the personal touch is still important. Etiquette expert Kim Izzo advises, "Taking that extra bit of time to write a thank-you note really means everything."

BIBLE**TRUTH** 3

The leper did not let social pressure restrain his gratitude. LUKE 17:17-19

■ **Why might the Samaritan leper have felt embarrassed to express gratitude? How might peer pressure discourage us from showing gratitude?**

INSIDE STORY: Samaritans were members of a race produced when Jews intermarried with Gentiles. Jews considered Samaritans unworthy to associate with (John 4:9) and even used the term *Samaritan* as an all-purpose insult (John 8:48). Jesus expressed amazement that the only person to offer proper thanks was the leper one would least expect to do so! It would have been the easiest thing in the world for the Samaritan leper to continue on with his Jewish fellow-lepers. But he stood against the crowd and expressed thanksgiving. In an increasingly uncivil world, Christians need to be counter-cultural in our expressions of thanksgiving.

CHALLENGE

Saying thanks does not necessarily require a lot of words. Close this session with a prayer time that illustrates this. Open the group prayer time thanking God for his blessings. Encourage students to pray aloud by simply speaking one-word prayers. Each student can pray by naming a particular blessing for which he or she is grateful.

INSTANT **STUDY** 15 ... CONTINUED

Copyright © 2009 Standard Publishing. All rights reserved. Permission to photocopy for ministry purposes only—not for resale.

The Pharisee and the Tax Collector

AS WE APPROACH GOD IN PRAYER, WE NEED TO BE SURE OUR HEARTS ARE RIGHT.

Request Denied!

Some people just can't wait to go to college! With obvious enthusiasm, a student prepared an application to Eastern Illinois University. But because of the way the information was presented, the package received a very different reaction than was intended.

Between 10:30 and 11 AM on a summer day, an alarmed mail carrier contacted the Facilities, Planning, and Management Department of Eastern Illinois University. The carrier was concerned about a suspicious package addressed to the college's admissions office. The university immediately contacted the county emergency services department.

Tom Watson, Coles County Emergency Management Agency coordinator, said the envelope appeared to be suspicious for a number of reasons. "It was a normal envelope but it was very thick," Watson said. "It had no return address. There were stains on it, and the mailing address was misspelled. [The mail carrier] did exactly what she was supposed to do."

The local fire department cordoned off the area around the Facilities, Planning, and Management building, blocking the street as a safety precaution. Employees in the area were sent home early. Assistant Chief Pat Goodwin of the Charleston Fire and Rescue Department reported that the postmaster from the city from which the package originated was contacted. The Illinois Secretary of State Police's bomb squad X-rayed the envelope. The package that simply contained a college application was finally verified to be safe around 3:30 that afternoon.

On the following day, Vicki Woodard, a spokeswoman for Eastern Illinois University, gave an official statement about the incident to the press. Woodward, however, would not comment when asked whether or not the bomb scare would affect the prospective student's chances of admission.

QUESTIONS TO CONSIDER:

■ Review the preceding article. List some reasons that the package in question appeared to be suspicious. If you were going to prepare a college application, why is this case a good example of things not to do when sending an important document to someone?

■ How did this application reveal more information about the applicant than was intended? How likely, in your opinion, is it that this student's application will be accepted? Why? Can you think of other times in which the way a request is delivered is as important as the request itself?

■ It seems that this college application revealed too much information about the student submitting it. Incomplete information, a stained envelope, and misspelled words would probably be interpreted as signs that the applicant lacked the skills and self-discipline to be a successful college student.

■ The Bible tells us that sometimes our prayers to God reveal too much information about ourselves because of the way we present them to God. Let's examine a parable in which Jesus compares the prayers of two different men "applying" for God's favor.

INSTANT **STUDY 16** ■ NEW **TESTAMENT**

37

Copyright © 2009 Standard Publishing. All rights reserved. Permission to photocopy for ministry purposes only—not for resale.

BIBLE**TRUTH** 1

God does not want us to tell him how we compare to others. LUKE 18:11

■ **How did the Pharisee compare himself to others? What was wrong about this prayer?**

INSIDE STORY: Everybody in Jesus' audience knew the Pharisees were the good guys. For nearly two hundred years they had been fighting to keep the influence of the pagan nations out of Israel. They kept God's laws better than anyone—and they knew it! The bad guy in Jesus' story would obviously be the tax collector. He not only rubbed elbows with the infidel Romans; he actually worked for them!

The Pharisee in Jesus' parable prayed at the proper hours for prayer (mid-morning, mid-afternoon, and sunset). Standing tall (the usual posture of public prayer for Jews), the Pharisee prayed mainly about himself and compared his piety to the overt sin of others (v. 11).

The apostle Paul was one of those Pharisees with an impressive line of spiritual credentials (Philippians 3:4-6). Yet after becoming a Christian, Paul realized that all such comparisons were meaningless "compared to the surpassing greatness of knowing Christ Jesus my Lord" (Philippians 3:8).

BIBLE**TRUTH** 2

God does not want us to report our good deeds to him. LUKE 18:12

■ **Why is it foolish to believe that human acts of worship impress God?**

INSIDE STORY: The Pharisee reported his perfect record of fasting and his scrupulous attention to tithing. This Pharisee seemed to be waiting for God to thank him for his great contribution to his kingdom. This false view that God should be grateful for the contributions of his followers can become a part of nearly any religion. When Paul was preaching to a totally pagan audience in Athens, he ridiculed them for trying to please their gods by building ornate temples and idols (Acts 17:25). God is not impressed by our feeble efforts at pleasing him.

At the end of his life, Leonardo da Vinci also recognized this truth. Though he spent his life creating unrivaled works of art, his final words on his deathbed were, "I have offended God and mankind because my work did not reach the quality it should have." Our best works can never impress the great God we serve.

BIBLE**TRUTH** 3

God wants us to approach him humbly, asking for mercy. LUKE 18:13, 14

■ **Contrast the two prayers in this parable. Which prayer do our prayers most resemble? Explain.**

INSIDE STORY: The tax collector stood in marked contrast to the pious Pharisee. He felt his guilt so keenly that he could not look up to Heaven—he could not look God in the face. In repentant sorrow the tax collector beat his breast. "God," he pleaded, "have mercy on me, a sinner" (v. 13). He had no defense, so he threw himself on the mercy of the court. He was a bad guy, and he knew it.

So what was the verdict? Only one man was declared "just" or innocent in God's eyes, and it was the tax collector (v. 14). The bottom line to this parable is this: Do we want to look good in our own eyes or in the eyes of God? If we are proud and exalt ourselves, we will be humiliated in the end. But if we humble ourselves in repentance, God will be ready to forgive.

CHALLENGE

Distribute pens and paper. Have students write letters of confession to God. Ask them to take them home so they can continue to throw themselves on the mercy of the divine court throughout the coming week.

Copyright © 2009 Standard Publishing. All rights reserved. Permission to photocopy for ministry purposes only—not for resale.

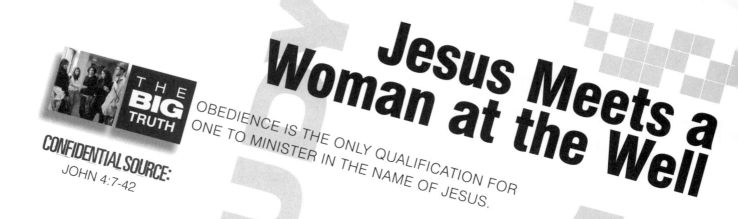

THE **BIG** TRUTH

CONFIDENTIAL SOURCE:
JOHN 4:7-42

OBEDIENCE IS THE ONLY QUALIFICATION FOR ONE TO MINISTER IN THE NAME OF JESUS.

Jesus Meets a Woman at the Well

Five Minutes of Fame

The Radio Music Awards are given annually for the best songs on mainstream radio. Although they are not the most highly sought-after music awards, winners graciously thank the radio industry and the fans that listen. They also make sure to commend their managers and record labels that help them attain stardom. Along the way, some artists thank God for giving them their talents. Sometimes they try to use the moment to promote new albums or express opinions on political and social issues. Like all awards programs, it reminds us that others have talents that most do not.

Thank-you speeches are interesting to watch. In just a handful of seconds, stars try to cram in everyone's name that helped them get to the top of their field. It's intriguing to see who gets priority on their lists. Whom do they consider to be integral to their success? Will they remember the fans whose adoration put them there in the first place? Sometimes winners don't seem all that grateful. Other times, their happiness is overwhelming, especially at the more famous award ceremonies. Consider these exuberant thank-you speeches from Academy Award winners:

• **When Cuba Gooding, Jr. won Best Actor in a Supporting Role in 1996 for the movie *Jerry Maguire*, he shouted and cried and hugged Tom Cruise and kept thanking people long past the orchestra's musical cue for him to conclude. His speech included the memorable phrase, "I love you, man."**

• **Roberto Benigni was overjoyed to accept awards for Best Actor in a Leading Role and Best Film in a Foreign Language in 1998 for the movie *Life is Beautiful*. In his Italian accent speaking broken English, he literally climbed onto the audience chairs with a huge grin and declared his love for America.**

• **In 2003, Adrien Brody was so excited to win Best Actor in a Leading Role for the movie *The Pianist* that he planted a big kiss on a very surprised Halle Berry who had just read his name and handed him the Oscar.**

Award shows come and go. Some are big and others are relatively small. But we will have our own moments of honor and our own thank-you speeches to give in life. Even when we are given the smallest of honor we can take that recognition as an affirmation that we have qualifications and talents that others don't have.

QUESTIONS TO CONSIDER:

■ Think about the last award show you watched. Did you agree that all of the winners should have gotten the awards? Did some people win who didn't seem as talented? Were some people who didn't win more qualified for the awards? Explain.

■ Do you ever watch award ceremonies and wish you were one of the winners? If you could win any award that exists, what would it be? Are you currently qualified to win that award? If not, what would you need to work on to be qualified? If you could make up an award that you are currently qualified to win, what would it be?

■ Sometimes we look at famous people and feel discouraged when we can't do the things they can. But even though we may not have their tremendous skills, we do have a job we're qualified to do—spreading God's Word. Yes, God can use any of us to share the love of Jesus. Today we're going to read about a very unlikely evangelist who ministered in the name of Jesus.

INSTANT**STUDY 17** ■ NEW**TESTAMENT**

Copyright © 2009 Standard Publishing. All rights reserved. Permission to photocopy for ministry purposes only—not for resale.

BIBLE TRUTHS

BIBLE**TRUTH** 1

The woman at the well was an unlikely evangelist because of her race and gender. JOHN 4:7-9

■ **What forms of discrimination have you witnessed? Why do you think it is wrong?**

INSIDE STORY: When Samaria, the capital of the northern kingdom, fell to the Assyrians, many of the Jews were deported to Assyria (2 Kings 17:4-6). To keep the land of Samaria fruitful, foreigners were sent to settle the land (2 Kings 17:24). As interracial marriages occurred between the foreigners and remaining Jews, the Jews from the southern kingdom rejected these mixed-race Samaritans as impure.

Imagine the Samaritan woman's shock when she turned to see who was asking her for a drink. Surely the Jewish man was making a mistake! This was also the reaction of Jesus' disciples who came back to find Jesus talking to a Samaritan woman in broad daylight (John 4:27). Jesus knew that by speaking to this woman, great things would happen. By talking to the Samaritan woman, Jesus was crossing boundaries. Jesus was showing that God's love is for every race and gender.

BIBLE**TRUTH** 2

The woman at the well was an unlikely evangelist because of her immoral lifestyle. JOHN 4:16-18

■ **Think of someone who you would be really surprised to see in church. Are they beyond God's ability to save? Explain.**

INSIDE STORY: Most women in Samaria retrieved their water in the morning and at the end of the day. This woman chose to get her water in the noonday heat (v. 6). As we read about her sexual history (v. 18), it seems obvious that she saw herself as an outcast among the other women of the community. The Samaritan woman needed some water, but because of her status as an outcast, she chose to go about getting it in a discreet way.

When the Samaritan woman arrived at the well, Jesus told her about water that would keep her from being thirsty again (vv. 10, 13, 14). That had to be intriguing to a woman who went out of her way to fetch water. But when the woman asked to be given the water, she had to admit her moral flaws to Jesus. Five husbands and living with a man to whom she wasn't married! What respectable man would want to associate with such an immoral woman? Jesus. Not only was he talking to a Samaritan woman, but also she was immoral. She was a woman who could truly understand what it was to need unconditional love.

BIBLE**TRUTH** 3

The woman at the well was a successful evangelist because she shared her knowledge of Jesus with others. JOHN 4:28-30, 39-42

■ **Excitement can be contagious. When have you been infected by someone else's enthusiasm?**

INSIDE STORY: The Samaritan woman was so touched by her encounter with Jesus that she ran off, leaving her water jar at the well. The woman never had a second thought about talking to those who had rejected her—she just knew that she had to share her story. The people were so intrigued by her excitement that *they sought Jesus.*

In today's culture it can be difficult to stand up for Christ and maintain respectable character. As a cast member of the reality TV show *Survivor*, Rodger Bingham did just that. Throughout the competition and gossip, Rodger remained a man of integrity that much of America came to respect. Even after being voted off the show, Rodger remained a grateful and humble man—one who will stick in many people's minds as what it really means to be a Christian. The great thing is that Rodger evangelized by being himself, plain and simple.

CHALLENGE: Many talent surveys are available online. Use or adapt one of those or create your own to help teens find their unique qualifications for ministry.

Copyright © 2009 Standard Publishing. All rights reserved. Permission to photocopy for ministry purposes only—not for resale.

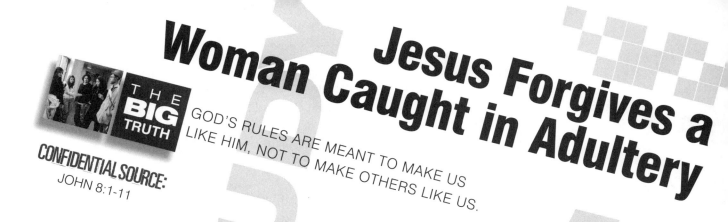

Jesus Forgives a Woman Caught in Adultery

THE BIG TRUTH

GOD'S RULES ARE MEANT TO MAKE US LIKE HIM, NOT TO MAKE OTHERS LIKE US.

CONFIDENTIAL SOURCE:
JOHN 8:1-11

Portraits of False Piety

One dictionary defines *self-righteous* as "piously sure of one's own moral goodness, especially when contrasted to the perceived evil of others." These news stories may serve to illustrate that definition.

- **We're rude . . . so what?!**—In a survey sponsored by the Dutch newspaper, *De Telegraaf*, Dutch citizens graded citizens of European countries on their manners. Readers determined that the Swiss, the Scandinavians, and the Belgians were Europe's most polite citizens. Surprisingly, the Dutch saw themselves as among the rudest people in Europe, third only to the Russians and the French.

  Yet that admission seems to have prompted more excuses than promises for change. In the words of one reader, "The Dutch are very direct in the way they communicate. Sometimes that's considered the same as being bad mannered."

- **A law for everyone else?**—Washington was rocked with scandal when Congressman Mark Foley of Florida suddenly resigned. Allegations that Foley sent sexually explicit messages to an underage Congressional page prompted the resignation and an investigation by the U. S. Attorney General.

  Especially troubling is the fact that Foley was Chairman of the House Caucus on Missing and Exploited Children and authored a large part of Child Protection and Safety Act of 2006. That law increased the penalties for the very offense that Foley was accused of committing.

- **Dealing with the "devil"**—In a speech before the United Nations, Venezuelan leader Hugo Chavez caused quite a stir. Chavez referred to the president of the United States as "the devil" who leads a "world dictatorship" and the U.S. government as being "imperialistic, fascist . . . and genocidal."

  Yet it is the money of the United States that fuels the Venezuelan economy. The U.S. purchases one and a half million barrels of oil each day from Chavez's nation. Chavez seems to have no problem taking money from the country he loves to hate!

QUESTIONS TO CONSIDER:

■ Choose one of the three news stories mentioned above. Why might someone call the behavior described in the article as *self-righteous?* What are some other examples of self-righteousness that you have seen in current events?

■ How can one identify a self-righteous person? What is that person's attitude toward others? Tell about a time when you felt that someone was exhibiting self-righteous behavior toward you. How did it make you feel?

■ Self-righteous people are all around us. But it is easy to fall into the trap of being self-righteous. It is easy to make ourselves feel that our sins are not as big of a deal as the sins of other people. It is easy to feel that we are morally superior to many. Let's see what we can learn from a time when Jesus confronted self-righteousness in his day.

Copyright © 2009 Standard Publishing. All rights reserved. Permission to photocopy for ministry purposes only—not for resale.

BIBLE TRUTHS

With Jesus involved, we can be assured that the law is always applied consistently. However, in today's legal system, those with more money than the average citizen seem to get off more easily than others who may not have the same influence. Thankfully, this is not the measure by which Jesus applied the law.

BIBLE**TRUTH** 1

Jesus examined motives for law keeping.

JOHN 8:1-6A

■ **Why do people obey laws? Give both good and bad motives for law keeping. How have you seen laws or rules used to manipulate others?**

INSIDE STORY: Laws are necessary to maintain order in society. The laws of biblical times were no different. According to the law of Moses, the punishment for adultery in Jesus' time was death by stoning (Leviticus 20:10). When the Pharisees brought the woman accused of adultery to Jesus, they were not concerned with keeping moral order, however. They were trying to trap Jesus, using this woman as a pawn.

Unlike the Pharisees, Jesus respected the law and the purpose for it. He refused to allow the law to be manipulated for the personal gain of others.

In today's society, people are often caught making false accusations against other individuals or corporations in pursuit of achieving their personal interests. The self-righteous still manipulate the law to their own ends.

BIBLE**TRUTH** 2

Jesus applied the law consistently. JOHN 8:6B-9

■ **Why do you think the woman, and not her partner, was brought before Jesus? How do you see rules applied inconsistently even today?**

INSIDE STORY: Jesus was not only fully aware of the woman's sin, but he also knew of the sins of the Pharisees and the others surrounding him in the temple. If the woman was to be stoned for her sin as the law stated, Jesus indicated that everyone should remain accountable for his or her sins. Like those surrounding Jesus that day, there is not one of us who is without sin and able to pick up that first stone. Realizing this, we must be careful about judging and condemning others' shortcomings without remaining accountable for our own.

BIBLE**TRUTH** 3

Jesus sought to help people rather than control them. JOHN 8:10, 11

■ **Contrast the idea of discipline used to help someone with discipline used to control someone.**

INSIDE STORY: Jesus, unlike the upright and holy Pharisees, cared about the "who" more than the "what" when it came to sin. He sought to help a sinner rather than merely punish one. He offered forgiveness instead of condemnation for the woman caught in adultery. With his nonjudgmental attitude, Jesus offered this woman the opportunity to start over with a clean slate and turn from her life of sin. It is through Jesus that we have this opportunity for forgiveness and a second chance. We don't know how this woman chose to live her life after her encounter with Jesus, but we can choose to follow Jesus' commands and change our ways as we leave our sins behind.

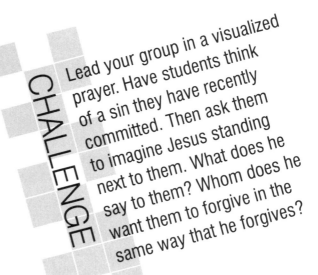

CHALLENGE Lead your group in a visualized prayer. Have students think of a sin they have recently committed. Then ask them to imagine Jesus standing next to them. What does he say to them? Whom does he want them to forgive in the same way that he forgives?

INSTANT**STUDY 18** ... CONTINUED

42

Copyright © 2009 Standard Publishing. All rights reserved. Permission to photocopy for ministry purposes only—not for resale.

Jesus Teaches about Serving Others

THE BIG TRUTH

A LIFE OF SERVICE IS THE HIGHEST OF CALLINGS.

CONFIDENTIAL SOURCE:
JOHN 13:3-17

Whom Do They Serve?

Some people choose jobs in which they are called to unselfishly serve the public. The news often tells of such people.

Abuse of trust—After the death of actress Anna Nicole Smith, one sensational story followed another. One revolved around photos that appeared in a Bahamas newspaper showing Immigration Minister Shane Gibson embracing Smith. This led to allegations that Gibson used his position of government service to grant special privileges to the actress known for her indulgent lifestyle.

After the photos were published, Gibson presented his resignation to Prime Minister Perry Christie. "I want to apologize to all persons who may in any way have been offended by anything that I have said, done, or perceived to have said or done," Gibson said in his televised resignation. "To the extent that my beloved country has in any way suffered . . . I want to apologize to the Bahamian people as a whole."

Search and rescue—Three climbers, two women and a man, fell from a snowy ledge of Oregon's Mount Hood. This prompted rescue teams into action. About thirty rescuers in all braved seventy-mile-per-hour winds on that same night to climb 8,300 feet up the 11,239-foot mountain. Rescuers camped out on Mount Hood and set out at daybreak the next day, hoping to beat a snowstorm expected later that day. Because they were able to talk to the climbers by cell phone and to determine their general location with their GPS device, rescuers were kept aware of their location and condition.

"They [the rescuers] are on the move," said Russell Gubele, coordinator of the operation. Despite a "very severe avalanche danger," he said, rescuers planned to "blanket that canyon" in search of the climbers.

Black Eye for JetBlue—Many travelers with reservations on JetBlue Airways were left stranded in New York's Kennedy Airport on Valentine's Day. Weather caused JetBlue flights to be cancelled in and out of eleven airports.

Cancellations continued through the beginning of the following week. Some travelers were further put out when baggage handlers could not find their bags in the mountains of accumulated luggage.

David G. Neeleman, the company's founder and chief executive, said that he was "humiliated and mortified" by the breakdown in the airline's operations and promised that the company would pay penalties if customers were stranded for too long. Neeleman said the crisis was the result of poor communications and reservation systems.

QUESTIONS TO CONSIDER:

■ Consider the news stories above. What does each one say about people in service occupations? Which people in these stories do you consider to be outstanding servants? Which fall short, in your opinion? Why?

■ What are some attitudes people have toward those in service-oriented occupations? What do you believe is the source of some of those feelings? What jobs would you be unwilling to take?

■ The job of serving others can be difficult, but Jesus tells us and shows us what kind of servants he wants his followers to be.

Copyright © 2009 Standard Publishing. All rights reserved. Permission to photocopy for ministry purposes only—not for resale.

BIBLE TRUTHS

BIBLE**TRUTH** 1

Service does not diminish a person's authority or worth. JOHN 13:3, 4, 12, 13

■ **What does it mean to you that Jesus was willing to do a servant's dirty job?**

INSIDE STORY: Though aware of his authority (John 13:3), Jesus nevertheless chose to act as the lowliest of servants. That is what a truly great person chooses to do. Earlier on the road to Jerusalem, Jesus lectured on servant leadership (Matthew 20:26-28). During the Last Supper, Jesus illustrated that lecture. The dusty roads of Palestine made the job of foot washing unpleasant, but Jesus assumed both the dress and the role of a slave (John 13:4).

After his act of service, Jesus asked his disciples, "Do you understand what I have done for you?" (v. 12). He began his answer to this question by acknowledging his place as both "Teacher" and "Lord" in their lives (v. 13). Service did not lessen Jesus' position, nor will it lessen ours. Jesus retained his divine status and ultimate glory, even though he "made himself nothing" (Philippians 2:7).

BIBLE**TRUTH** 2

Service is leadership by example. JOHN 13:14-16

■ **How could you follow Jesus' example and become more of a servant to others?**

INSIDE STORY: Jesus came to serve, but he also calls us to follow his example and serve one another with the same humility he showed (John 13:14, 15). Jesus has every right to give such a charge. After all, no underlings are ever greater than their bosses. If he was willing to serve his disciples, his disciples should have no excuse for not adopting the same mindset toward one another (v. 16). While some Christians have seen this as a command to institute a religious ritual, it appears to be much more. It is a call for an attitude that should mark the church as different from any other institution in the world.

Later Jesus would command Peter to "Feed [his] sheep" (John 21:17). When writing to elders of congregations in Asia Minor, Peter commanded that his fellow church leaders willingly assume that same role of servant (1 Peter 5:2). Unlike rulers or businessmen who lead for monetary gain or for the thrill of power, Christians who lead do so for the purpose of reflecting the example of Jesus to others (v. 3).

BIBLE**TRUTH** 3

Service is the only route to true happiness in life. JOHN 13:17

■ **How does the idea that serving others is the way to happiness conflict with what most people believe?**

Jesus ended his object lesson by saying that those who practiced this lesson would be "blessed" (John 13:17). Today most people believe that taking care of oneself, not others, is the prescription for happiness. The Bible clearly teaches that complete joy can only be found through working for others. Joy is complete when we celebrate what God has done and give him an offering of "the work of [our] hands" (Deuteronomy 16:15). Joy is completed when we obey Jesus, even to the point of giving our own lives (John 15:9-13). Joy is full when brothers and sisters in Christ live sacrificially for one another (Philippians 2:1-3).

CHALLENGE

American poet Edwin Arlington Robinson wrote poems describing the personality of certain people. Two of his poems stand in stark contrast to one another. "Richard Cory" tells of a self-serving and ultimately very unhappy man, whereas "Cliff Klingenhagen" tells of a happy man with a servant's heart. Before the lesson, obtain a copy of these two poems from your library or from these Internet addresses: http://www.bartleby.com/233/221.html and http://www.bartleby.com/104/45.html/ Read each poem or allow volunteers to do so. Then ask students to compare and contrast the messages of the poems to the Bible lesson. Ask them to consider the elements in their lives that make them a Richard Cory or a Cliff Klingenhagen and how they might alter their behavior in order to follow Christ more closely.

Copyright © 2009 Standard Publishing. All rights reserved. Permission to photocopy for ministry purposes only—not for resale.

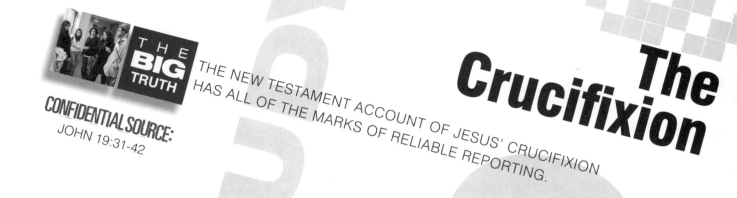

THE BIG TRUTH

CONFIDENTIAL SOURCE:
JOHN 19:31-42

THE NEW TESTAMENT ACCOUNT OF JESUS' CRUCIFIXION HAS ALL OF THE MARKS OF RELIABLE REPORTING.

The Crucifixion

Bogus Biography

The *New York Times* called her story a "remarkable book . . . [bearing] witness to the life in the 'hood that she escaped." The newspaper raved, "Ms. Jones's portraits of her family and friends are so sympathetic and unsentimental, so raw and tender and tough-minded, that it's clear to the reader that whatever detachment she learned as a child did not impair her capacity for caring." A week later the same publication called *Love and Consequences* "a complete fabrication."

Love and Consequences was released as a nonfiction title. The book was supposed to be a memoir by Margaret P. Jones, who described growing up as a half-white, half-Native-American foster child in gang-plagued Los Angeles. A few days later the truth was revealed. Margaret B. Jones is really Margaret "Peggy" Seltzer. Seltzer is not a former gang member of Native-American heritage. She did not grow up ducking bullets in South Central Los Angeles, getting her education on the streets. Rather, Seltzer grew up in suburban, solidly middle-class Sherman Oaks, California, and attended a private school.

This is not the first time fiction has masqueraded as nonfiction. In 1997, *Misha: A Memoire of the Holocaust Years* hit the bookshelves. The book claimed to be a true story of a Jewish refugee who escaped from the Nazis and was adopted by a pack of friendly wolves. The author, it was discovered, was not a refugee and not even Jewish. And there were no wolves.

In 1996, fiction writer Jeremiah "Terminator" LeRoy appeared on the literary scene. Although LeRoy wrote fiction, he claimed that his books revealed the truth of his life as an HIV-infected, homeless drug addict and male prostitute.

Nearly a decade later, LeRoy turned out to be Laura Albert, a healthy, well-to-do middle-aged mother. A friend of Albert, fashion designer Savannah Knoop, played the part of LeRoy by wearing an elaborate disguise during public appearances.

So why does this happen? How have phony tales of the dark side of society been passed off as truth? Television writer David Mills *(Homicide, The Corner, ER, The Wire)* suggests that the blame lies with book editors. Mills argues that the largely white, upper-middle-class editors responsible for acquiring books for publication are nearly illiterate when it comes to life on the mean streets.

QUESTIONS TO CONSIDER:

■ What do you think about these controversial books or others like them? Why do you believe so many people who should know better are fooled like this?

■ What are some examples of false stories being passed off as the real thing? (Consider supermarket tabloids and Internet rumors, for example.) What are some ways we can discover whether or not such claims are true?

■ We are continually sorting through what we are told, deciding what is trustworthy and what is dubious at best. That includes questions about God and faith. Many religions make truth claims that are no more reliable that those of Margaret Seltzer. Today we will examine one of the most important accounts in Scripture—the crucifixion of Christ. How can we know whether or not this narrative is truly history, as it claims to be?

Copyright © 2009 Standard Publishing. All rights reserved. Permission to photocopy for ministry purposes only—not for resale.

BIBLE TRUTHS

BIBLE**TRUTH** 1

Jesus' execution was performed by the ruling powers of the day. JOHN 19:31-34

■ Could you write an accurate account of life in the Old West? Why not? What might the historical accuracy of an account say about the one who wrote it?

INSIDE STORY: The apostle John records the terrible scene of Jesus' crucifixion with historical details. The event took place during the Roman occupation of Israel, during the reign of Tiberius, and on the Friday preceding the Jewish feast of Passover. Each of these times, people, and places can be found in other historical documents. John also gives authentic details of the interaction between Jews and Romans. Because the next day after Jesus' crucifixion was the Sabbath of the Passover feast, the Jewish leaders asked Pilate to have his soldiers speed the death of those on the crosses by breaking their legs. That way the bodies could be taken down before sundown, the beginning of the Sabbath. It was the general custom of the Romans to allow crucified criminals to remain on their crosses for days. Jewish law, however, required that an executed criminal's body not be left unburied overnight (Deuteronomy 21:22, 23). All of these details are the stuff of history, not fable.

BIBLE**TRUTH** 2

Jesus' execution was consistent with centuries-old prophecy. JOHN 19:35-37

■ Tell about a time when you said, "I knew that would happen."

INSIDE STORY: John is careful to note that he is a truthful eyewitness and that what was happening to Jesus was the fulfillment of prophecies recorded long before. The unbroken bones tied Jesus to the Paschal lamb whose blood had been shed as a part of the deliverance from the bondage of Egypt (Exodus 12:1-30, 46; Numbers 9:11, 12) and the pierced body hearkened back to Zechariah 12:10. John is the only

Gospel writer who mentions the piercing spear and the blood and water coming from Jesus' side. Because the culture to which John wrote was influenced by mysticism, he makes every effort to show that Jesus was flesh and blood and literally died on that cross. Furthermore, the blood and water flowing from the side prefigure the important Christian ordinances of communion and baptism.

BIBLE**TRUTH** 3

Jesus' burial was consistent with the customs of the day. JOHN 19:38-42

■ Do you know someone from a foreign country? What are some American customs that are unfamiliar to that person?

INSIDE STORY: Both Joseph of Arimathea and Nicodemus were secret followers of Jesus. Both were men of importance. It took courage to ask Pilate's permission to take down and bury the body of Jesus. They took the body to Joseph of Arimathea's nearby rock-cut tomb. Such tombs generally consisted of a large chamber, with smaller chambers for individual bodies opening from it. Often, many bodies were placed in such tombs, but this one had never been used before. John continues supplying details of the burial, describing the nature of the shroud and the types and amount of embalming spice. Again, we see a logical correlation of custom, social status, and practice that one would not see in myth.

CHALLENGE

Before the lesson, paint a cross on several pennies so each student may have one. Have them put that penny with the rest of their loose change in a pocket or purse. Challenge them to think of the change the crucifixion of Christ should make in their lives when they see that penny among their pocket change throughout next week.

INSTANT **STUDY 20** ... CONTINUED

Copyright © 2009 Standard Publishing. All rights reserved. Permission to photocopy for ministry purposes only—not for resale.

THE BIG TRUTH

CONFIDENTIAL SOURCE:
ACTS 1:1-5; 2:1-39

THE SAME GOD WHO WAS AT WORK IN THE BIRTH OF THE CHURCH WORKS IN THE CHURCH TODAY.

The Church Begins

Name Game

"Where do you go to school?" "Dummer Academy."

You can just imagine the giggles, snickers, and snorts in reaction to the historic boarding school in Newbury, Massachusetts. Because of the comical sounding name, the school's board of trustees decided to change it.

"Rightly or wrongly, first impressions make a difference," said headmaster John M. Doggett, explaining the name change (or as he called it, the "name refinement"). "Certainly, when you go outside of the Boston region, the first impression sometimes doesn't convey what the school is all about."

The name does not seem to have hurt the school's reputation too badly. Last year there were 100 openings in the school and 800 students applied. Currently there are 371 total students paying around $33,000 a year to attend.

Boston Globe columnist Brian McGrory objected to the name change. "What the [school's] trustees are telling the rest of the world is that it's all about conforming to the needs of the market and correctly positioning your institution in this competitive global climate. . . . They're saying that image is more important than tradition, that conformity is the way of the day, that the path of least resistance is the road best traveled."

So what's with that funny sounding name anyway? Governor Dummer Academy, which claims to be the oldest boarding school in the nation, is named after eighteenth century Massachusetts governor William Dummer. Governor Dummer donated some of his land to start the school in 1763. In its history, the school has maintained a prestigious clientele—Paul Revere created the school's seal and John Quincy Adams was once secretary of the board of trustees.

Now the name of the school is simply The Governor's Academy. The school hopes that the new name preserves the history of the school without making it a punch line.

QUESTIONS TO CONSIDER:

■ When you read the first paragraph and saw the name Dummer Academy, how did you react? Do you think the history of the school's name should have affected the board of trustees' decision? If you were on the board, would you have changed the school's name? Defend your answers.

■ In understanding things such as funny names, it helps to go back to the beginning and find out why things were created. For instance, if we want to have a more complete understanding of what the church is all about, we need to look back at the beginning of it. Today we're going see how God established his church.

Copyright © 2009 Standard Publishing. All rights reserved. Permission to photocopy for ministry purposes only—not for resale.

BIBLE TRUTHS

BIBLE**TRUTH** 1

After his resurrection, Jesus continued to teach his disciples about founding his church.
ACTS 1:1-5

■ **If people were asked to identify the key message of Christianity, what would they say? Are they right?**

INSIDE STORY: Between the resurrection and his ascension (40 forty days later), Jesus gave his disciples "convincing proofs" that he was alive again—appearing among them, talking with them, eating, and letting them touch him (Acts 1:3). Since the resurrection would be the cornerstone of the apostolic message, Jesus wanted there to be no doubt to the truth of this event (1 Corinthians 15:1-6, 14). During that time Jesus gave further "instructions through the Holy Spirit," (Acts 1:2) which included the commands to preach to all nations (Matthew 28:18-20; Mark 16:15-19; Luke 24:45-49) and further explanation of the kingdom of God. The apostles were told not to worry about the lingering popular hope for a restored earthly kingdom. Their job was to get busy spreading the gospel (Acts 1:6, 7). The promised coming of the Holy Spirit (Joel 2:28-32) would empower them and help them as they began in Jerusalem and spread outward into Judea, Samaria, and the rest of the world (Acts 1:8). The apostles were required to wait in Jerusalem a few more days for the Spirit (vv. 4, 5). The church today should be clearly teaching what Jesus wanted his apostles to know during those forty days after the resurrection.

BIBLE**TRUTH** 2

God poured out his power on the disciples in a miraculous way. ACTS 2:1-6

■ **Give an example of how a display of power draws attention. Does your church draw other's attention?**

INSIDE STORY: Pentecost is one of the three annual feasts of Judaism (Deuteronomy 16), coming fifty days after Passover.

Faithful Jews from all over the world would go to Jerusalem for Passover and stay until Pentecost. When the Holy Spirit empowered the apostles to speak in the native languages of the crowd, people "came together in bewilderment" (Acts 2:6). Now that the power of God had gotten the crowd's attention, Peter offered an explanation. What they were seeing was the beginning of the long-awaited fulfillment of Joel's prediction about the coming of the Holy Spirit to all mankind (Joel 2:28-32). The world today may not have a right to expect tongues of flame, but they should be able to see miraculous evidence of the Spirit of God working in changed lives, restored families, and healthy relationships that they do not regularly see elsewhere.

BIBLE**TRUTH** 3

Peter introduced thousands to the church with a sermon. ACTS 2:12-14, 16, 17, 22-24, 36-39

■ **What are some ways groups call people to take action? What call to action should the church offer?**

INSIDE STORY: Peter continued, reviewing the ministry of Jesus, his miracles, and his death, burial, and resurrection. Remember, most of this crowd was in Jerusalem two months earlier. Many present then were among that crowd that called for Jesus' crucifixion! Conviction and fear gripped those who realized that they had rejected the very one they were waiting for (v. 37). Peter's response simply echoed what Jesus had commanded in the Great Commission—preach the gospel, with belief, repentance, and baptism as the necessary human responses. Repentance and immersion in Christ's name result in forgiveness and reception of the promised Spirit (v. 38). The church today must also be marked by its emphasis on evangelism. The good news the apostles shared is the same good news we have as well.

CHALLENGE
Write the words Educate, Empower, and Evangelize on the board. Ask students to give examples of how they can perform these actions that were a part of the first church.

Copyright © 2009 Standard Publishing. All rights reserved. Permission to photocopy for ministry purposes only—not for resale.

TODAY'S CHURCH NEEDS TO COPY THE HEALTHY HABITS SEEN IN THE EARLY CHURCH.

The Church's Practices

In Another World

Is too much media consumption unhealthy? A recent poll of 3,000 teens by a British cable channel yielded some unsettling results to that question.

UKTV Gold features "classic" TV programs from England and the U.S. such as *Fawlty Towers, Dr. Who, Fantasy Island, Baywatch,* and *Charlie's Angels*. The fifteen-year-old channel is roughly the equivalent of Nickelodeon's TV Land in the U.S. Their recent survey attempted to better understand what British teens (who have watched this channel most of their lives) know about basic historical facts.

The survey indicated that teens acquire their historical knowledge primarily through entertainment media. (Similar conclusions were made by a recent Harvard University study in the U.S. that showed that teens were more likely to gain political information from entertainment programs such as *The Colbert Report* or *The Daily Show with Jon Stewart* than from actual news sources.) More than three-quarters of those polled by UKTV (77 percent) admitted they did not read history books, and 61 percent said that they changed channels rather than watch historical programs on television.

As a result, teens surveyed were shockingly unable to distinguish between fantasy and reality in many cases. When asked to tell whether a specific person was real or mythological, UK teens were frighteningly uninformed. Almost a quarter of the respondents (23 percent) believe that World War II British Prime Minister Winston Churchill, who has often been hailed as "the greatest Briton of all time," was made up. The survey found that 47 percent think that Richard the Lionheart, the twelfth-century English king and commander during the Crusades, was a myth. A significant percentage considered Indian political leader Mahatma Gandhi of the twentieth century to be a fictional character.

On the other hand, many fictional characters are believed to be real. Almost two-thirds (65 percent) believe that King Arthur and his Knights of the Round Table actually existed. Nearly as many (58 percent) believe fictional detective Sherlock Holmes to be real. Around half of those surveyed believe that the lonely title character of the Beatles's song "Eleanor Rigby" (47 percent) and mythological archer Robin Hood (51 percent) were actual people.

"While there's no excuse for demoting real historical figures such as Churchill, the elevation of mythical figures to real life shows the impact good films could have in shaping the public consciousness," said Paul Moreton, the head of UKTV Gold.

QUESTIONS TO CONSIDER:

■ How do you react to the results of the UKTV Gold survey? How do you believe teens you know would answer the same questions? What might be some results of these misunderstandings?

■ Experts agree that being able to distinguish reality from fantasy is essential to good mental health. For that reason, they worry about the mental health of the British teens that took the survey. What are some other signs of mentally *unhealthy* people or societies? What are some signs of people or societies who are mentally *healthy*?

■ The Bible describes the early church as a mentally and spiritually healthy community. Let's examine God's Word to discover some characteristics that made them so.

INSTANT**STUDY 22** ■ NEW**TESTAMENT**

Copyright © 2009 Standard Publishing. All rights reserved. Permission to photocopy for ministry purposes only—not for resale.

BIBLE TRUTHS

BIBLE**TRUTH** 1

The early church spent time studying the revealed Word of God. ACTS 2:42; 4:32, 33

■ **How would the world be different if all Bibles disappeared tomorrow? Would that change your life? Explain.**

INSIDE STORY: The early church was "devoted . . . to the apostles' teaching" (Acts 2:42). The fact that the apostles actually saw who Jesus was and what he did forms a refrain through the apostolic writings (1 Corinthians 15:5-8; 2 Peter 1:16; 1 John 1:1). Dedication to the Word of God revealed by reliable eyewitnesses caused the early church to be "one in heart and mind" (Acts 4:32) and to be united into one joyful body (1 John 1: 3, 4). Hunger for God's Word reminds us that "man does not live on bread alone but on every word that comes from the mouth of the LORD" (Deuteronomy 8:3), and these words are "sweeter than honey to my mouth" (Psalm 119:103)! Peter compared the believer's desire for God's Word to the hunger of a newborn infant for nourishing milk (1 Peter 2:2, 3).

BIBLE**TRUTH** 2

The early church spent time sharing their lives with one another. ACTS 2:42, 44, 45; 4:32, 34, 35

■ **What does the word *fellowship* mean to you?**

INSIDE STORY: Fellowship is more than sharing a dinner together. It is becoming a single entity, sharing together in weakness and strength (Acts 2:42, 1 Corinthians 12:26). Biblically, fellowship is two-fold. It is a "fellowship with us" (other believers) and a "fellowship...with the Father and with his Son" (1 John 1:3). This is "the fellowship of the Holy Spirit" (2 Corinthians 13:14). Biblical fellowship is "being united with Christ" and then "being one in spirit and purpose" (Philippians 2:1, 2). With that dual fellowship, we dedicate ourselves "to the interests of others" (v. 4). The church of Jerusalem expressed this fellowship by selling their possessions and giving the income to the apostles to be distributed to meet the needs of all of these believers (Acts 2:44, 45; 4:32, 34, 35). There is no indication that this was done outside of the church in Jerusalem, but congregations of believers in other locations used other means to share generously with one another (Acts 11:27-30; 1 Corinthians 16:1, 2; Philippians 4:14-16). The method of sharing is not as important as the act of sharing.

BIBLE**TRUTH** 3

The early church spent time worshiping God. ACTS 2:42, 43, 46, 47

■ **What do you think is most important when we worship? What did the early church do?**

INSIDE STORY: The first believers were "devoted . . . to the breaking of bread and to prayer" (Acts 2:42). Meaningful, expressive worship is a mark of a healthy church. "Breaking of bread" referred to the fellowship of sharing common meals, to be sure. But these fellowship feasts also included the memorial and ceremonial meal of Communion, the Lord's Supper. In it, believers remember the sacrifice of Jesus and pledge to await his return with brothers and sisters in the faith (Matthew 26:26-29; 1 Corinthians 11:23-29). Prayer was also a vital part of worship. These prayers were pleas to God for strength and intervention. For example, after Peter and John were imprisoned and tried for their faith, the response of the church was prayer for boldness as believers continued to preach the Word of God. This act of worship was so powerful that God literally shook the physical structure in which they met (Acts 4:23-31)!

CHALLENGE Give each student a short length of wire. Challenge them to create a symbol representing Bible study, fellowship, or worship that will remind them of a practice in their life they most need to strengthen.

INSTANT **STUDY** 22 ... CONTINUED

Copyright © 2009 Standard Publishing. All rights reserved. Permission to photocopy for ministry purposes only—not for resale.

THE BIG TRUTH

CONFIDENTIAL SOURCE:
ACTS 6:8-15; 7:51–8:2

WE MUST BE WILLING TO SPEAK OUT ABOUT GOD NO MATTER THE COST.

Stephen Is Martyred

The Problem of Pain

You read it, watch it, and hear about it in the news every day—suffering. Many people suffer, but why? The reasons for most suffering could fit into three categories: the person's sin, other people's sins, or accidental circumstances. Here are three examples.

Example one: the person's sin

Paul Shanley, a former priest who was defrocked by the Vatican, was sentenced to a prison term of twelve to fifteen years. Shanley was convicted of raping and molesting a boy in the 1980s. Several others had accused Shanley of similar actions but did not want to testify. Shanley would be eligible for parole after he serves at least two-thirds of his sentence time, but his lawyer is worried that seventy-four-year-old Shanley will likely die in prison "given his age and frailty."

Example two: other people's sins

A seventy-four-year-old American nun was murdered in Brazil's Amazon jungles. Sister Dorothy Stang had worked in the area for over thirty years, caring for the poor and defending peasant farmers who are being driven from their land by ruthless loggers and ranchers. Before she died, Sister Dorothy pulled out her Bible and began reading to the two gunmen. They paused for a few moments and then shot her. Many loggers and ranchers in the area, who often occupied the land illegally, strongly disliked Sister Dorothy. In fact, many people sent her death threats, and those who worked with Sister Dorothy believe she knew she would be killed soon.

Example three: accidental circumstances

An explosion inside a Chinese mine killed 203 workers, injured twenty-two others, and trapped twelve underground. This was the deadliest mining accident in China in over fifty years. China has had a nationwide safety campaign to prevent such tragedies. Despite that, there are still more deaths in Chinese mines than any other mines in the world. Here are some statistics: Of all mining deaths in the world, 80 percent happen in China. About 6,000 people die in floods, explosions, and fires that occurred in mines each year. The worst mine accident ever happened in China in 1942, when 1,549 people died.

QUESTIONS TO CONSIDER:

■ Name other examples of suffering you've seen in the news lately that fit into these three categories. Name an example of suffering from your own life that fits into one of these categories.

■ Is suffering fair? Can suffering bring good results? Explain your responses.

■ Today we will read about Stephen, an early church leader who died because he shared his faith. Let's see what role unjust suffering has in God's plan.

Copyright © 2009 Standard Publishing. All rights reserved. Permission to photocopy for ministry purposes only—not for resale.

BIBLE TRUTHS

BIBLE**TRUTH** 1

Stephen was a righteous man. ACTS 6:8, 10, 15

■ **It is generally true that good things happen to good people. What exceptions to that have you seen?**

INSIDE STORY: Stephen was chosen along with six others to meet the needs of the Grecian widows in the church (Acts 6:1-6). But despite Stephen's character, some opposed his message. Because they could not refute his arguments, these men resorted to legal action. When Stephen was brought before the Sanhedrin to stand trial, his godly character was so obvious that "his face was like the face of an angel" to his accusers (v. 15).

The Union of Myanmar (Burma) has historically denied religious freedom. In one Burmese village there is a man of godly character named Timothy. He spoke boldly to the soldiers who came to destroy his village telling them, "Only this book [the Bible] can deliver freedom for our people." That day eleven soldiers came forward for prayer and three were baptized in the river. Godly men and women still present powerful arguments for Jesus.

BIBLE**TRUTH** 2

Those who rejected God plotted to destroy Stephen. ACTS 6:9, 11-14

■ **When have you seen a person who could not win an argument resort to dishonesty?**

INSIDE STORY: Frustrated by Stephen's powerful arguments, his opponents arranged for false testimony against him. This resulted in a trial before the Sanhedrin, the ruling council of the Jews. Stephen had claimed that the worship of God would no longer be restricted to the temple (Acts 7:48-50). But his accusers twisted those words into a statement in opposition to God, the temple, and Moses. Nevertheless, Stephen maintained his composure.

While Myanmar does not claim any official religion, the Burmese government uses its power to favor Buddhism.

Known as the State Peace and Development Council (SPDC), the Burmese army burns villages—many times attacking churches first and then destroying homes and crops. All too often, the SPDC attacks any villager who does not have time to escape, beheading the men, raping the women, and taking the children and forcing them to become soldiers. The powerful continue to conspire to silence the message of Christ.

BIBLE**TRUTH** 3

Stephen's character did not spare him from negative consequences. ACTS 7:51–8:2

■ **Why would God allow someone to suffer unjustly?**

INSIDE STORY: Before the Sanhedrin, Stephen demonstrated from Scripture that Jewish leaders had consistently fought God's plan throughout their history. This brought a furious response (v. 54). Their anger was heightened when Stephen, under the guidance of the Holy Spirit, announced that he could "see heaven open and the Son of Man standing at the right hand of God" (vv. 55, 56). In their refusal to hear any more of Stephen's words, they executed him. Moments before his death Stephen asked the Lord to receive his spirit and forgive his murderers for their sins. Saul, who later became a Christian convert and apostle, witnessed Stephen's stoning and gave full approval to his death. Stephen's murder sparked a great persecution of the church. As believers mourned his death and buried his body, other believers were forced to flee from the growing persecution (Acts 8:1b, 2).

Persecution of the church did not stop in Stephen's day. In fact, more Christians have been killed for their faith in the past century than in all of the other centuries of church history combined.

CHALLENGE Have each student write a short list of people they know they should tell more about Jesus. Next to each name, challenge them to write the fear that keeps them from doing so. Pray together for courage.

Copyright © 2009 Standard Publishing. All rights reserved. Permission to photocopy for ministry purposes only—not for resale.

GOD'S KINGDOM IS AVAILABLE TO ALL WHO ACCEPT HIM.

CONFIDENTIAL SOURCE:
ACTS 10:1-48

The First Gentile Christians

Overlooked Christians

Does Hollywood represent the average American? An example can be seen in the case of the film, *The Passion of the Christ*. Director Mel Gibson had a hard time finding anyone to produce the film. No one thought a movie about faith would be successful. Then the film became one of the top moneymaking movies of 2004. Nevertheless, it does not appear on most film critics' "best movies of 2004" lists. Nor was it in contention for a "Best Picture" Oscar. Perhaps the critics in Hollywood think the movie is for conservative viewers only. And *conservative* is a more negative word in Hollywood today than it has been in years.

"Most movies are absolutely non-political," said movie critic Michael Medved. "My criticism of the entertainment industry would be that when they do send political messages, it is always, always from the left." He pointed out that scripts are changed to fit the tone of Hollywood, even when books are made into movies. Medved said that when Hollywood made conservative Tom Clancy's book *Sum of All Fears* into a movie, the bad guys were changed to fit a different set of politics. Similarly, the entire plot of John Grisham's *The Runaway Jury* was changed from a tobacco case to a gun law case when it went to film.

"The point is that when it comes to overt messages, liberals send those messages all the time and very often are praised for them," Medved continued. "There are no movies in the recent past that send overt unapologetic conservative messages. Why? Because anybody who attempted to do that would be criticized [and] ostracized socially, if not commercially, in the Hollywood community."

James Hirsen, with conservative NewsMax.com, said people in the movie industry are scared to let people know they are conservative. "There is this weird new definition of 'tolerance' in Hollywood. We are only tolerant to those that agree with us. Which is not, of course, tolerance at all."

Screenwriter Lionel Chetwynd said that conservatives in the movie business must prove their skills before they express their views. Otherwise, he said, conservative filmmakers will be overlooked.

Screenwriter Craig Titley said, "Where else in this country can you be a conservative and it's the equivalent of Marlon Brando in a leather jacket riding into town? Like we're the rebel counterculture, the nonconformists. Everywhere else in the country if you're conservative, you're the square."

QUESTIONS TO CONSIDER:

■ Do you agree that Hollywood films are biased against conservative or Christian values? Defend your answer with a specific example or two. Do you know any organizations or media that seem biased against socially liberal views? Explain.

■ Name a time when you stereotyped people or their ideas before you got to know them. How were your first impressions wrong? What's the danger of categorizing people?

■ We place people into categories without even noticing it. But that can lead to stereotypes and judgmental attitudes that misrepresent who people really are on the inside. Peter had to face his own judgments about people. God showed Peter that his kingdom is offered to everyone.

Copyright © 2009 Standard Publishing. All rights reserved. Permission to photocopy for ministry purposes only—not for resale.

BIBLE TRUTHS

BIBLE**TRUTH** 1

God seeks people from every nation. ACTS 10:1-4

■ **Who do you know that honestly seeks God but might feel uncomfortable at your church? Why?**

INSIDE STORY: Cornelius was a successful soldier of Rome (v. 1). But more importantly, Cornelius was an honest seeker of God (v. 2). In the book of Acts we read of other "God-fearing" people like Cornelius, those who were not Jews but worshiped in the Jewish synagogue (13:50; 16:14; 17:4; 17:17; 18:7). Nevertheless, they were excluded from Judaism and, at one point, the church because they were not ethnically Jewish.

Cornelius's acts of worship also included regular prayer and giving. But there was no human institution to which he could belong to corporately worship the God of Israel. God intervened by sending an angel (10:3). In this way, God told Cornelius that his acts of worship were not going unnoticed. God would prepare a place for him in his church (v. 4).

BIBLE**TRUTH** 2

God enlists workers to invite others to God.
ACTS 10:9-20

■ **Can you think of Christians who have been called to minister to outcasts? Name some of them.**

INSIDE STORY: God brings messengers and seekers together. Cornelius was told to send for Peter at Joppa. God then went to Peter to prepare him for his callers. Peter, hungry and praying, had a vision concerning unclean foods (vv. 9-14). By his initial reaction, we can safely infer that the animals he saw and was commanded to kill and eat were from the lists of unclean and forbidden food (Leviticus 11 and Deuteronomy 14:1-21). However, the repeated message of the vision was "what God has declared clean is no longer unclean"

(Acts 10:15). While Peter would have to think through this, it meant the removal of cultural barriers between Jews and Gentiles that had been created by the Mosaic law. At this point, Cornelius's men arrived and the Holy Spirit advised Peter to welcome and accompany them so as to share the message with the one who had sent them (vv. 17-20).

BIBLE**TRUTH** 3

God brings people to himself by his power.
ACTS 10:24-48

■ **What are the most successful missionary efforts you know about? What makes them successful?**

INSIDE STORY: When Peter arrived, Cornelius had gathered family and friends to greet the apostle (v. 24). Upon hearing how the angel told Cornelius to send for him and after sharing the lesson of his own vision, Peter came to the conclusion that God plays no favorites. When honest seekers of God are brought together with his humble servants, God takes over! The coming of the Holy Spirit on Pentecost was reenacted among the Gentiles gathered there (vv. 44-46a). Because God's acceptance of the Gentiles was obvious to Peter and the other Jews with him, they baptized Cornelius, his family, and his friends in the name of Jesus (vv. 47, 48).

Christians taking the message of Christ into mainland China, as well as Christians who live in that country have suffered horribly. Yet some estimate that there are an average of 28,000 people every day who make a commitment to follow Jesus in China. When those who seek God connect with servants sent by God, the power of the gospel is evident!

CHALLENGE Spend some time brainstorming ways students can get involved in one of the missionary efforts your church supports. Bring in materials that describe these missions and what needs they have.

INSTANT**STUDY 24** . . . CONTINUED

Copyright © 2009 Standard Publishing. All rights reserved. Permission to photocopy for ministry purposes only—not for resale.

THE BIG TRUTH

CONFIDENTIAL SOURCE:
ACTS 16:16-34

WE NEED TO TAKE ADVANTAGE OF EVERY OPPORTUNITY TO SHARE THE GOOD NEWS.

Opportunities in Philippi

Too Busy to Shop

If you just found out that you won a contest prize of over $7,000 for a shopping spree, what would your reaction be? Would you say, "No thanks. I'm too busy right now"? Probably not! But that's what a woman from Spain said recently.

A woman, whose name is not known, entered the "La Compra-Reloj" *(shopping against the clock)* competition held by the Chamber of Commerce in the city of Murcia, Spain. The contest involved 600 stores and was organized to boost local small businesses. More than 60,000 people entered the contest. The winner was to receive 6,000 euros for a shopping extravaganza with a three-hour time limit.

When the event's organizers called the lady to share the great news that she had won, she told them she'd have to think about it. Then she never showed up to collect her winnings. A spokesperson for the event quoted the woman as saying she was "too busy to waste the morning."

So instead, the prize went to twenty-eight-year-old Piedad López García , the runner-up contestant. Ms. Garcia made the most of the opportunity. In slightly more than two hours on a Friday, she purchased jewelry, clothes, shoes, home décor, sunglasses, presents for her family, and a whole ham.

QUESTIONS TO CONSIDER:

■ What's your first reaction after reading this story? What do you think of the first woman's choice? Why do you think she passed up on such a fun opportunity?

■ What would you have done in if you had won the shopping spree? What do you think Piedad López García thought about the woman's decision?

■ Have you ever missed out on a great opportunity because you were too busy? Describe the situation. How did you feel once you found out what you missed?

■ Have you ever missed an opportunity to do something nice for someone else? (Ex: not helping when someone was struggling to carry something; not taking time to listen when a friend was having a bad day; not taking time to give directions to a new student who was lost on his first day at school; not visiting your grandparents very often; etc.) Describe the opportunity you missed. How could you avoid opportunities like that in the future?

■ When we pass up an opportunity to participate in something great, we end up regretting it later. Today we'll read about Paul and Silas, who were not afraid to share the gospel when an opportunity came their way.

INSTANT**STUDY 25** ■ NEW**TESTAMENT**

55

Copyright © 2009 Standard Publishing. All rights reserved. Permission to photocopy for ministry purposes only—not for resale.

BIBLE TRUTHS

BIBLE**TRUTH** 1

Allow for interruptions. ACTS 16:16-18

■ **Whom in your life do you consider to be a pest? What might that person *really* want from you?**

INSIDE STORY: Once when going again to a place of prayer, Paul met a slave girl who had an evil spirit that allowed her to predict the future. Her owners made a nice profit from her abilities (Acts 16:16). Like the demonic spirits who recognized Jesus (Mark 1:24; 5:7), this spirit caused the girl to recognize and proclaim that Paul was a messenger of God (Acts 16:17). She followed Paul for many days, shouting loudly to everyone. Exasperated at this uninvited publicity, Paul finally turned and cast the spirit out of her (v. 18).

Jesus told two parables about people who made nuisances of themselves. A visitor kept pounding on the door of his friend's house until he received provisions (Luke 11:5-8). A widow kept petitioning a judge until he gave her justice (18:1-5). In Philippi, Paul stopped to notice that the girl he considered a nuisance was a person in need. Instead of continuing to ignore her and to be irritated, Paul acted with compassion.

BIBLE**TRUTH** 2

Praise God despite problems. ACTS 16:19-25

■ **How do problems affect your attitude? How does your attitude affect your behavior?**

INSIDE STORY: The angry owners dragged Paul and Silas into the marketplace to face the authorities (Acts 16:19). They charged Paul and Silas with an uproar by advocating non-Roman customs, but the real issue was the anger of the owners at losing the opportunity to enslave someone for their own profit. Spurred on by a noisy crowd, the magistrates ordered Paul and Silas to be stripped and beaten with wooden rods the size of broom handles, and then forced them to sit spread-eagled with their feet in stocks (vv. 22-24).

What could they do when it's midnight and they hurt too bad to sleep? Sing, of course! Paul and Silas prayed and sang praises to God while the other prisoners listened (v. 25). One could only imagine what they thought! Suddenly, an earthquake shook the jail. All the doors flew open and everyone's chains fell off. In Philippi, Paul found opportunities to share the gospel with inmates and his jailer by praising God in the midst of trouble.

BIBLE**TRUTH** 3

Look beyond surface questions to real needs.
ACTS 16:26, 29-34

■ **Have you ever asked for junk food when you really needed a full meal? Think of other situations when people might ask for something other than what they really need.**

INSIDE STORY: If a prisoner escaped, the guard would receive that prisoner's punishment—even death (Acts 12:18, 19). When the jailor asked how to be saved, it is possible that he could have simply been saying, "How do I get out of this mess!" But Paul recognized that the guard's real issues were spiritual ones. Therefore Paul answered the real question with the real answer. Faith—trust in and faithfulness to Christ—is the basis of salvation (John 3:16). The jailer listened as Paul preached the word of the Lord. In that same hour, even though it was the middle of the night, the jailer and his family were baptized (Acts 16:33). By not being tied to superficial questions and by giving biblical answers, Paul took an opportunity that ended in real joy for an entire family (v. 34).

CHALLENGE Create a chain of dominoes and knock one over. Explain how taking advantage of opportunities God has for us is like that—one thing leads to another. Give each student a domino to remind them to look for opportunities God gives them.

Copyright © 2009 Standard Publishing. All rights reserved. Permission to photocopy for ministry purposes only—not for resale.

WE GIVE ANSWERS TO OTHERS, WE NEED TO UNDERSTAND THEIR QUESTIONS.

Correcting Misunderstandings

Com U ni C8

"2 B r nt 2 B?" Could this question be the answer when your English teacher asks for the famous first line of Hamlet's soliloquy? Perhaps, if a recent decision in New Zealand makes its way to this country.

Recently New Zealand's Qualifications Authority (NZQA), the country's department of education, announced that students would not be penalized if they use text-speak in answering questions on school exams. While it still strongly discourages students from using anything other than full English, credit will be given if the answer "clearly shows the required understanding," even if it contains text-speak.

Text-speak, the use of abbreviated words and phrases such as *lol* for *laughing out loud, IMO* for *in my opinion*, and *CU L8R* for *see you later*, is widely used by those of us who communicate digitally through cell phone text messages or instant messaging providers.

In the minds of some educators, using these types of abbreviations is just another method of communication. Students should still aim to make their answers as clear as possible, said Bali Haque, the deputy chief executive for qualifications in the NZQA. Debbie Te Whaiti, the Post Primary Teachers' Association President, said the NZQA's decision simply reflects the way teens communicate.

Others, however, respond with, "R U c RE us?" They are concerned that use of text-speak could lead to misunderstandings and problems. Blogger (the word itself being an abbreviation denoting someone who writes a *Web log*) Tony Hung speculates, "I'm having a hard time telling if this represents exactly how technologically advanced New Zealand is, or, if it (like the introduction of Ebonics in some schools in the States) represents yet another milestone in the decline of Western Civilization." Fellow blogger Alex Rosenleaf asks, "Are we really so lazy as to purchase our rest at the cost of degraded language?" A retired teacher writes, "They did what . . . ? This cannot be; I haven't been out of the game long enough for things to have fallen to such a pass. My red pen is poised; my red hair is standing on end."

Rosenleaf challenges students not to use this shortcut. "Do not take advantage of what your educational overlords are offering. You can use vowels! You can use consonants! You can use them together!"

QUESTIONS TO CONSIDER:

■ How often do you use text-speak? Would you consider using it to answer questions on a test in school? Why or why not? On the back of this paper, list as many text-speak abbreviations as you can. Try to think of a few messages written in text-speak that may be easily misunderstood. What problems might occur if those messages failed to communicate clearly?

■ Unclear communication is just one reason why misunderstandings may occur. Think of a time when you had an argument with someone because of a misunderstanding.

■ Misunderstandings occur when someone does not have a clear grasp of the words or facts used by another. Today we will look at a misunderstanding that occurred in the early church because there was not a clear understanding about what it meant to be a Christian. Let's see how that misunderstanding was corrected.

INSTANT **STUDY 26** ■ NEW **TESTAMENT**

57

Copyright © 2009 Standard Publishing. All rights reserved. Permission to photocopy for ministry purposes only—not for resale.

BIBLE TRUTHS

BIBLE**TRUTH** 1

Paul corrected believers who held to false doctrine. ACTS 19:1-7

■ **Why do you think Christians disagree about important issues at times? How should we respond?**

INSIDE STORY: In Ephesus, Paul encountered a dozen men who had received only the baptism of repentance preached by John. These disciples didn't have a full understanding of the completed work of Christ, the granting of the Holy Spirit (Mark 1:8). It appears that Apollos had taught these men before Priscilla and Aquila corrected him (Acts 18:24-26). While the message to repent is solidly part of the gospel, it is only a part. Without having the Holy Spirit's power to live what their repentance promised, those believers in Ephesus would have known a religion of empty works and frustration. Therefore, Paul preached the whole gospel to these men.

Even today many claim Jesus while holding to false teaching. Polls tell us that 53 percent of teens believe that Jesus sinned while on earth and 60 percent believe that one can go to Heaven by doing good deeds. Like Paul did, we need to respond to them with clear correction.

BIBLE**TRUTH** 2

Paul answered unbelievers as long as they asked honest questions. ACTS 19:8, 9A

■ **Do you know someone who just likes to argue? What is the best way to deal with that person?**

INSIDE STORY: In Ephesus, Paul began his ministry in a synagogue, as was his customary practice. This is a pattern he followed throughout his missionary journeys (Acts 13:14; 14:1; 17:2, 10; 18:4). He certainly taught that Jesus fulfilled the law and reconciles both Jews and Gentiles to God through his sacrifice (Ephesians 2:11-22). This certainly would have raised questions from the Jews who zealously guarded their special covenant with God.

For three months, the Jews asked these questions (Acts 19:8). Paul surely understood their confusion, since he was also a Jew, in fact, a Pharisee. As long as the Jews sought the truth, he was glad to give honest answers. However, when they refused to accept it and began to malign the message, Paul left the synagogue (v. 9a).

As long as questions from unbelievers are fair and honest, answers should be given. Yet when seekers no longer seek truth but only want to win an argument, it is best to move on.

BIBLE**TRUTH** 3

Paul led sincere disciples into a deeper understanding of God's will. ACTS 19:9B, 10

■ **How do shallow conversations differ from deep ones? What does having deep conversations require?**

INSIDE STORY: Paul took from the synagogue the disciples who truly wanted to hear his message and set up shop in a rented lecture hall (19:9b). In two years of such teaching, Paul certainly brought many listeners to a deeper understanding, far beyond simply knowing the tenets of the faith (v. 10). The rest of the story indicates that not only did the listeners become believers, but they also turned away from evil practices such as sorcery (vv. 11-20). The presentation of the gospel does not stop after one first becomes a Christian. Rather, we are called to take hungry, young believers and "leave the elementary teachings about Christ and go on to maturity" (Hebrews 6:1).

CHALLENGE: Give each student a piece of paper and have him or her divide friends and acquaintances into these three categories: those who know just a bit about Christianity, those who know nothing and ask questions, and those who know some but want to know more and grow. Encourage students to recognize these differences and think of strategies for talking to each group about Jesus.

Copyright © 2009 Standard Publishing. All rights reserved. Permission to photocopy for ministry purposes only—not for resale.

JESUS ROSE FROM THE DEAD, JUST AS HE SAID HE WOULD.

CONFIDENTIAL SOURCE:
1 CORINTHIANS 15:1-8

The Resurrection

Preseason Predictions

Every year before the season starts for Major League Baseball (MLB), sportswriters begin the baseball season by making a number of predictions of how the sport will look 162 games later. These journalists weigh in with their picks for Rookie of the Year, Most Valuable Player, and who they pick to win the World Series.

So how reliable are preseason predictions? Consider the track record of Hall of Fame baseball reporter Peter Gammons. Gammons is arguably one of the very best in his field, having been voted the National Sportswriter of the Year for 1989, 1990, and 1993 by the National Sportscasters and Sportswriters. Here are Gammon's picks for World Champion for six consecutive years compared to what really happened:

- **2003**—Gammons predicted Oakland would defeat Arizona in the World Series. In actuality, the Los Angeles Angels beat the San Francisco Giants.
- **2004**—Gammons saw Chicago Cubs beating the Boston Red Sox. In October, it was Boston over the St. Louis Cardinals.
- **2005**—Gammons picked the Minnesota Twins over the Cubs. In fact, the Chicago White Sox defeated the Houston Astros.
- **2006**—Gammons favored the New York Yankees over the St. Louis Cardinals. The Cardinals took the crown over the Detroit Tigers that year.
- **2007**—Gammons predicted that the Tigers would best the New York Mets. Instead, Boston defeated the Colorado Rockies for the title.

- **2008**—Gammons predicted that the Cleveland Indians would take it all by defeating the Atlanta Braves in October. As it turned out, neither team even made it to the playoffs! The Indians finished seven and a half games out of first place and the Braves were twenty games back.

"Predictions have no currency," admits Gammons. "They are non-fiction, radio-TV shock-jock stuff."

QUESTIONS TO CONSIDER:

■ What do you think Peter Gammons meant when he wrote, "Predictions have no currency"? Do you pay much attention to baseball (or other sports) predictions? Why? What are some bases upon which experts make such predictions?

■ What are some other areas in which predictions are made? (For example, consider political polling or weather forecasts.) Tell about any type of recent prediction that did not come true. Why do you think that those predictions were unreliable?

■ Gammons admits that baseball predictions have more entertainment value than reliability. Many predictions are like that. But such faulty predictions help us appreciate someone who is consistently right in his or her predictions. Let's examine some predictions made about Jesus and the resurrection to see how reliable those predictions were.

INSTANT**STUDY 27** ■ NEW**TESTAMENT**

59

Copyright © 2009 Standard Publishing. All rights reserved. Permission to photocopy for ministry purposes only—not for resale.

BIBLE TRUTHS

BIBLE**TRUTH** 1

We know Jesus rose from the dead because he still changes lives. 1 CORINTHIANS 15:1, 2

■ **Who do you know whose life has been changed by becoming a Christian? How has it changed?**

INSIDE STORY: Paul reminded the Corinthians that the resurrected Christ empowers believers to live changed lives (1 Corinthians 15:1). Earlier in this same letter, Paul reviewed with the Corinthian Christians the sins of people all around them (6:9, 10). But Paul ended this list with a note of hope: "and that is what some of you were" (v. 11). Some of the greatest evidence of Jesus' resurrection was the many lives that Paul had seen changed because of Jesus. Paul had seen God blind the eyes of a powerful political advisor on the island of Cyprus, convincing the ruler there to follow Jesus (Acts 13:4-12). Paul witnessed a man from Lystra who had been lame since birth leap to his feet and walk (Acts 14:8-10). The risen Christ freed Paul and Silas from prison in Philippi (Acts 16:16-34). With those events fresh in his mind, surely Paul cited them as evidence that Jesus lives and works among those who seek him.

BIBLE**TRUTH** 2

We know Jesus rose from the dead because we trust the reliability of God's revelation.

1 CORINTHIANS 15:3, 4

■ **How often have you seen predictions not come true? What does it mean to you when they do come true?**

INSIDE STORY: Paul continued to defend the resurrection by saying it had been predicted in detail centuries before the fact (1 Corinthians 15:4). Isaiah spoke of a suffering servant pierced to take away our sorrows, pay for our transgressions, and heal the wounds brought by our sin (Isaiah 53:4-6, 10-12). Zechariah also predicted that a special servant of God would come and be "pierced" in Jerusalem (Zechariah 12:10). The stories of the Old Testament also contain many hints that one would come who would be saved from death

on the third day. Isaac, the only begotten son of Abraham (see Hebrews 11:17), was saved from death on the third day (Genesis 22:1-5, 12-14). King Hezekiah was diagnosed with a terminal disease but was healed on the third day (2 Kings 20:1-11). Just as Jesus would spend three days in a tomb and be released, Jonah spent three days entombed in the belly of a huge fish (Jonah 1:7-17; Matthew 12:40).

BIBLE **TRUTH** 3

We know Jesus rose from the dead because of independent eyewitness accounts.

1 CORINTHIANS 15:5-8

■ **When have you said, "I wouldn't have believed it if I hadn't seen it for myself"?**

INSIDE STORY: Paul listed witnesses who saw the risen Lord. Jesus appeared to the disciples (1 Corinthians 15:5) and to 500 or so other believers simultaneously. The Corinthians could even contact the witnesses and hear the stories themselves (v. 6)! Jesus appeared to his half-brother James and the rest of the apostolic circle, including Paul himself (vv. 7, 8). These were reliable people that the Corinthians either knew personally or by reputation. Furthermore, often those who saw Jesus were *not* expecting to see him. The men on the road to Emmaus walked miles with Jesus before recognizing him (Luke 24:13-35). Mary Magdalene first assumed that the person she saw at the tomb was a gardener (John 20:15). Thomas was convinced that Jesus had not been raised from the dead when Jesus appeared to him (John 20:24-28). Paul was actively persecuting the church, convinced that the resurrection of Jesus was a hoax (Acts 9:1-19). These sightings were not wish fulfillment!

CHALLENGE The resurrection changes everything. Challenge students to list things in their lives they won't need once they get to Heaven. These may be material things or attitudes that are unnecessary because of the resurrection.

Copyright © 2009 Standard Publishing. All rights reserved. Permission to photocopy for ministry purposes only—not for resale.

THE **BIG** TRUTH

CONFIDENTIAL SOURCE:
ROMANS 4:1-8

TRYING TO EARN GOD'S FAVOR IS FUTILE.

By Works or Faith?

Free or Fee?

Federal law demands that states provide free public education for students from kindergarten through high school. But in these days of tight budgets, school districts throughout the nation have developed a plan to go around the law and into the pockets of parents.

While the education remains free, supplies are not. During back-to-school time, parents are reaching into their wallets to pay textbook, materials, and activities fees. At Warren Western Reserve Middle School in Warren City, Ohio, parents are charged $15 for students taking physical education, $8 in lab fees for biology classes, and a $5 keyboarding fee for students using computers. In Southington, Ohio, parents must pay for workbooks and other instructional material that the school districts wouldn't be able to reuse. For first graders, that includes a charge of $31.50 for a math workbook, $3.75 for the *Weekly Reader,* and $20 for a language workbook. In Lawrence, Kansas, the textbook fee is $72 per year for each student, except kindergartners, who pay $36. Participation fees for sports and other extracurricular activities are $50 per student, and bus fees are $240 per year. Band students in New Orleans are charged a band fee of $20-40, and all students there must pay a locker rental fee.

"Charging fees is a practice the board has to enforce to live within its means," said Southington (Ohio) Superintendent Frank Danso. "I think in essence, we all have to live within a budget." "Fees are not unusual at all," commented Kansas Deputy Education Commissioner Dale Dennis. Lawrence (Kansas) school board president Sue Morgan explained that fees were implemented because for the past few years the state has made fewer tax dollars available to the schools. "It would be lovely if we could reach the point where we could roll some of these fees back, but our situation hasn't changed that much from the situation that pushed us to install the fees in the first place," she said.

But this means that parents must pay more for "free" public education. For Lori Nation, the mother of four students in Lawrence public schools, bus, textbook and activity fees set the family back about $1,000. "The fees are just getting out of control," Nation said. She and her husband, she said, are "still paying off last year's fees."

QUESTIONS TO CONSIDER:

■ Do you know if your school charges materials and activities fees? If so, what kinds of fees must be paid? According to the article, this plan puts a large burden on some parents. What do your parents think about these fees? Do you think they would ever refuse to pay those fees if it meant that you would not get as good of an education? Explain.

■ For a moment, make a mental list of things that your parents provide for you. Estimate how much money that costs them each year. What could they do with that money if they did not spend it on you? Why do you think they choose to sacrifice for you?

■ While book and activity fees may be an inconvenience for parents, most parents gladly make that sacrifice for their children. It is obvious that parental love does not require that children earn the sacrifices their parents have made for them. But sometimes we act as though we, as God's children, must earn his favor. Today we'll study his plan of salvation for us—a plan in which he sacrificially paid all of the cost involved!

Copyright © 2009 Standard Publishing. All rights reserved. Permission to photocopy for ministry purposes only—not for resale.

BIBLE TRUTHS

BIBLE**TRUTH** 1

Working for salvation is trying to prove that we deserve God's favor. ROMANS 4:4

■ **Many believe that people go to Heaven because they have done good things. What do you think and why?**

INSIDE STORY: Salvation is not a matter of gaining God's favor. While we live according to God's will, in his favor, there is no need for salvation. But we all have fallen out of God's favor (Romans 3:23).

When someone takes a job, he or she is agreeing to do specific tasks in return for specific wages (Romans 4:4). The employee deserves to be paid for the work but deserves to be fired when he or she doesn't do the job. When an employee is fired, there is usually nothing that can be done to earn back the job. The fact is, we broke the contract with God years ago. We were "fired." Working madly to prove we can earn God's love is just as pitiful as a fired employee working hard to receive a paycheck that will never come.

BIBLE**TRUTH** 2

Trusting God for salvation is believing that God will love us even though we are unworthy.
ROMANS 4:5

■ **If it only took one sinful act a day for God to reject you, about how many days a week would you be on God's good side?**

INSIDE STORY: Here is the good news! Salvation is separate from the law (Romans 3:21). While the law requires work and obedience, salvation is a gift (Romans 4:5). Workers who clock in and out every day rightfully expect their employer to give them a paycheck. But the panhandler on the sidewalk near the office building is another matter. The beggar only hopes that someone who has what he needs will give it to him freely.

Each of us is that beggar. God owes us nothing, but gives us everything. He does not dismiss our evil deeds as if we deserve to be forgiven. Rather, he created a way separate from the law to pay for our debts to him.

BIBLE**TRUTH** 3

The greatest heroes of the Old Testament knew that only faith, not works, could merit God's love.
ROMANS 4:1-3; 6-8

■ **Tell about a time when as a child you "helped" a parent do something, only to make a mess of things.**

INSIDE STORY: The Jews were expecting God to keep his promises of blessings to them because they were descendants of Abraham. But it is because of God's faithful nature that he keeps his promises, not because of adherence to the letter of the law. Two of the greatest heroes of the Old Testament, Abraham and David, knew that.

Abram was promised that he would be the father of a great nation. But at the time that promise was made, his wife was unable to have children. In a disastrous act of doubt and impatience, Abram decided to father a child by his wife's handmaiden Hagar. His attempt at "helping" God with that promise fathered the nations with whom Israel is at war to this day (Genesis 16:1-4, 12, 15, 16)! But God fulfilled his promise of offspring for Abram through his strength alone (Genesis 18:10-15; Genesis 21:1-7). Abraham learned that it was not his works that earned God's blessings, but his trust (Romans 4:3).

King David learned the same lesson. David understood that his position as King of Israel was one granted by grace and not earned (2 Samuel 7:18-29). Yet after years of military victories, he started thinking that his victories were the result of the mighty army the he had assembled, David took inventory of his fighting men. In trusting his works over God's grace, David brought disaster upon his nation (2 Samuel 24:1-17 or 1 Chronicles 21:1-17). As a result, David again came to know "God credits righteousness apart from works" (Romans 4:6).

CHALLENGE

Encourage students to write one of the following verses on a note card: Exodus 15:2; 1 Chronicles 16:23; Romans 5:8; Ephesians 1:17; or 2 Timothy 1:9. Challenge them to memorize it this week.

Copyright © 2009 Standard Publishing. All rights reserved. Permission to photocopy for ministry purposes only—not for resale.

THE BIG TRUTH

CONFIDENTIAL SOURCE:
ROMANS 5:12-21

WE ARE SAVED BY THE WORK OF JESUS AND NOT BY OBSERVING THE LAW.

About Law and Sin

Powerless

On August 14, 2003, the biggest blackout in North American history hit the northeast part of the country, covering 9,300 square miles and leaving fifty million people without power. This failure affected parts of eight states and two Canadian provinces and happened in under three minutes. Investigators immediately tried to fully answer the big question: Why?

After a massive blackout in 1965, a non-profit group called the North American Electric Reliability Council (NERC) formed to design a grid system that would prevent major outages. If a problem occurs, the system is supposed to shut it off from the rest of the grid, so the impact will be minimal and not cause "shock waves" that could generate multiple failures.

"There were fail-safe steps in place, and they didn't work. We don't know whether it's a faulty design or whether it's not following the rules," said NERC president Michehl Gent to CNN's Wolf Blitzer.

Several power lines owned by FirstEnergy Corp. in Ohio failed an hour before this major power outage, but the alarm that is supposed to warn operators of the problem did not go off. Because the problem was not isolated, it crossed the lines of the Eastern Interconnection, which links states in the Midwest and East. Yet Gent did not solely blame FirstEnergy. "This is much more complicated than just a few lines in Ohio or the control system at that utility," he continued.

Some documents were found that indicated that government and utility monitors such as the Federal Energy Regulatory Commission were concerned about the strain put on the Eastern Interconnection by huge increases in power used during the summertime. Quality control agencies in the power industry noticed more frequent problems on the lines in the past few years and urged utilities to be aware of the limits of the system. But investigators will have to determine what specific warnings were issued and to whom those warnings were given. This will also lead into a more thorough look at the various operating standards utility companies have across the country.

QUESTIONS
TO CONSIDER:

■ Were you ever affected by a power blackout? Describe the experience. How would a loss of electrical power for several hours affect the way you live?

■ What is NERC? When and why was the organization created?

■ Think about a time when you took a corrective action. Perhaps you tried to prevent an injury, cure an illness, or repair something, but failed. Why was your action ineffective?

■ Sometimes even the most elaborate plans made to solve problems fail. Sometimes plans fail because they are not followed. Sometimes plans fail because the problem is bigger than we imagine. The problem of sin is a problem that has been addressed by philosophers, social planners, and religious practitioners for centuries. But Paul tells us that we can only solve the problem if we note the *cause*, the *cure*, and the *consequences*.

Copyright © 2009 Standard Publishing. All rights reserved. Permission to photocopy for ministry purposes only—not for resale.

BIBLE TRUTHS

BIBLE **TRUTH** 1

Human beings are not sinners because they break the law; they break the law because they are sinners. ROMANS 5:12-17

■ **What is the difference between a *disease* and a *symptom*? Can we cure a disease by only treating symptoms? Explain.**

INSIDE STORY: Until Moses received the Commandments, there was no formal law. So how can it be true that "before the law was given, sin was in the world" (v. 13)? Paul explains that sin is as much of a "medical" problem as it is a "legal" problem. Many believe that we become sinners when we break the Ten Commandments, but this "legal" violation is only a symptom of the real problem. The "medical" problem is that through Adam all humanity is infected with an inclination toward sin (v. 12). That includes those who lived before the Ten Commandments were given (v. 14). Sin is not just a matter of what we have done; it is a matter of who we are—broken creations of God (Romans 7:15).

A pig is not just dirty because it wallows in mud. It wallows in mud because it is a pig! Until a pig's nature changes, it will be dirty (2 Peter 2:22). The old hymn, "Rock of Ages," refers to a similar fact. "Be of sin the *double cure*," writes the poet. "Cleanse me from its guilt and power." We not only need to be cleaned up from sins we commit, we also need to have our nature changed so that we will not race back to wallow in sin.

BIBLE**TRUTH** 2

Christians do not belong to Jesus because they are good; they are made good because they belong to Jesus. ROMANS 5:18, 19

■ **Tell about a time when someone did something for you when you could not do it yourself.**

INSIDE STORY: Imagine a four-person relay team when the first runner stumbles. The rest of the team had not even begun the race yet, but the entire team suffers the

consequences of the first runner's mistake. Now imagine that the coach jumps onto the track, picks up the baton, and continues the race. The second runner misses the hand-off, but the coach keeps running. The coach passes the remaining team members and quickly catches the rest of the pack, winning the race. At the awards ceremony each team member stands with a gold medal around his neck, giving credit to the coach. Just as the team would have lost because of the one misstep of the first teammate, it won with the sole effort of the coach. Likewise, salvation is "not from yourselves" (Ephesians 2:8). Members of the team called "Christians" are not winners because *they* won the race. They won the race because Jesus made them winners (Romans 5:19)!

BIBLE**TRUTH** 3

We can either despair because we can't keep the law or rejoice because Jesus is willing to keep it for us. ROMANS 5:20, 21

■ **List some differences between a person who sees a glass as half empty and one who sees the same glass as being half full.**

INSIDE STORY: "The law was added so that the trespass might increase" (v. 20a). In other words, the law serves to show how far broken human nature differs from God's holy nature. This can cause us to want to give up, knowing that we can never meet God's standards by our own efforts. Paul called this "the smell of death" (2 Corinthians 2:15, 16). "But where sin increased, grace increased all the more" (Romans 5:20b). Instead of focusing upon our weakness, we are called to focus upon God's generosity! The existence of the law is not a reason to be discouraged. It is a reason to praise a God of grace.

CHALLENGE

Illustrate the necessity of having sin removed before we can obey God by sprinkling salt on a table and placing a sheet of paper over it. With a ruler, try to draw a straight line, but note that the salt makes your best efforts futile. It is only when the sin (symbolized by the salt) is removed, we can live a "straight-line" life.

Copyright © 2009 Standard Publishing. All rights reserved. Permission to photocopy for ministry purposes only—not for resale.

From Salvation to Glorification

Bumpy Road to Forgiveness

Sometimes we can escape consequences of our words with a simple, "Pardon me." For Muslim villagers Najma Biwi and Sheikh Ershad from eastern India, the path from transgression to reconciliation was not nearly so straightforward.

Ershad shouted the word *talaq* three times to his wife Najma while he was drunk. The word *talaq* means divorce, and according to the Islamic clerics in the area, Ershad's words were all that were necessary to make the divorce official. The couple did not wish to divorce and continued to live together. Nevertheless, the local religious leaders heard about the case from the neighbors and insisted that the couple divorce.

According to religious law, the only way Biwi can reunite with her husband and their three children is to undergo what their law calls *Halala*. A wife divorced this way can only reunite with the husband who divorced her if she marries another man for at least one day and then divorces him. The man that the woman marries temporarily must be at least seventy years old according to the leaders.

At first the couple sought another route to get back together. They went to the State Women Commission, the state Human Rights Commission, and the National Human Rights Commission to ask them to overturn the decision of the religious council. The village leaders resisted, leaving the only alternatives to be a long legal fight or *Halala*. Last week Biwi and Ershad agreed to comply with the religious leaders.

"Two days before she is to remarry, the village committee members will finalize the person who will be bridegroom. Generally we select an old man to marry a divorced woman," explained Ayab Ali, a village committee member.

This process has not been uncommon in this part of India. Each year, between ten and twenty married women in this region have had to perform *Halala* to atone for their husbands' saying *talaq*, according to Ali.

QUESTIONS TO CONSIDER:

■ What is your opinion of this story? Do you think that this couple should have been permitted to stay together rather than go through the complicated process of divorce and remarriage followed by another divorce and remarriage? How should it have been handled? Defend your answer.

■ Ershad and Biwi thought that getting back together should have been a very straightforward affair. Nevertheless, the religious community made the path for them to get back together a complicated one. Have you ever been told a process or given directions that you thought were unnecessarily complicated? Tell about that.

■ The fact is, our sin divorces us from God. Sometimes people devise complicated religious schemes to bring us back together with God, but they are not effective. The Bible, on the other hand, tells us very clearly how God directs us on the path back to him. Let's look at what Paul says about this.

Copyright © 2009 Standard Publishing. All rights reserved. Permission to photocopy for ministry purposes only—not for resale.

BIBLE TRUTHS

BIBLE**TRUTH** 1

Salvation begins when we accept Christ and is complete when we are in Heaven. ROMANS 8:28-30

■ **Think about a trip you have taken. Describe both the destination and the events that occurred along the way.**

INSIDE STORY: Those who are saved are also "being saved." When we trust God for salvation, we begin a journey with him. The first step of the journey is that *God foreknew.* God knew that there would be people who loved him and created them to walk with him (Leviticus 26:12). Next, *God predestined.* Parents make plans before a child is born. They plan to give that unborn child life's necessities and direction and purpose. God made a plan so his children would grow up "to be conformed to the likeness of his Son" (Romans 8:29). Thirdly, *God called.* God offered his plan through his prophets, and ultimately by means of his Son. God's servants today continue to call people to accept his plan (Romans 10:14-17). Then *God justified.* God's plan, determined "before the creation of the world," was to make us "holy and blameless in his sight" through the sacrifice of his Son (Ephesians 1:4). Finally, *God glorified.* The plan will be complete when we pass from this life to the next (Romans 8:20, 21).

BIBLE**TRUTH** 2

God continues his work in us to bring us to maturity in Christ. ROMANS 8:31, 32

■ **You have been given a trip to Europe. Everything has been paid for except your way to get there. Why is that not enough?**

INSIDE STORY: There is a gap between when we accept God's plan of salvation and when his promise of heaven is finally fulfilled—the rest of our life on earth. We try to live godly lives, but are constantly struggling with temptation. Paul offers encouragement by saying, in effect, "OK, now that we know how much God loves us and to what lengths he has gone to secure a place for us in Heaven, why should

we worry about getting there? Don't you think that he would do whatever he could to help us reach the end?" God knows what we're facing. Jesus himself faced the same things, and now helps us when we are tempted (Hebrews 2:18). Although temptations are common for all people, God provides a way for us to endure them (1 Corinthians 10:13).

BIBLE**TRUTH** 3

No power outside of us can thwart God's work in us. ROMANS 8:33-39

■ **Imagine that two people are going on vacation, and one of them is a wanted fugitive. Who do you think will have the best time? Explain.**

INSIDE STORY: Paul uses an illustration of a courtroom. On trial is all of mankind. We have many accusers: our friends and family, Satan, and even God's own law. The accusation against us is that we have broken the law. And we are guilty (Romans 1:20; 3:10, 23; 5:12). But Paul also makes it clear that there is no one who can get a conviction against those who love God. Despite our sin, God's power enables him to make perfect those who love him through the death of Jesus. And it is Jesus who testifies for us at this trial!

God the judge can now rule on any charge that could come up against us. "I've lied to my parents, can God forgive that?" Yes. "I'm a teenage mom, can God forgive that?" Certainly. "I used to ridicule Christians and make fun of Jesus." God can forgive that. "So, what about my sins tomorrow?" For those who love God, he has taken care of all that and more. We are declared not guilty so we can make the trip to Heaven.

CHALLENGE

Have students label the lower left-hand corner of a sheet of paper "My Life Today Five Years Ago" and the upper right-hand corner of the paper "Heaven." Instruct the students to make maps of their own lives. Ask them to illustrate the side streets and detours they have made in their lives. Ask them to think about the future and what side streets and detours they could avoid.

INSTANT**STUDY** 30 ... CONTINUED

Copyright © 2009 Standard Publishing. All rights reserved. Permission to photocopy for ministry purposes only—not for resale.

Is Christianity Just Another Religion?

THE GOOD NEWS OF JESUS IS SUPERIOR TO MAN-MADE RELIGION.

CONFIDENTIAL SOURCE:
GALATIANS 1:6-24

Catching Counterfeits

For years the $100 bill has presented a temptation for counterfeiters. But recently added security measures now making it easy to spot false bills could thwart those who seek to make money by printing their own.

The "C-note" has long been a favorite bill to copy. More than 70 percent of the $776 billion of U.S. currency in circulation is in $100 bills. Since about two-thirds of these bills are held overseas, counterfeiters exist both in and out of our country. With the availability of ever-more sophisticated computers, scanners, and color copiers, security must become more high-tech than ever before.

By the end of 2008, new $100 bills produced with special security threads were scheduled to enter circulation. These security threads combined micro-printing with tiny lenses that magnified the micro-printing. About 650,000 lenses appear on a single $100 bill! As a result, when one moves a bill side to side, the image of Benjamin Franklin appears to move up and down. When one moves the bill up and down, the image appears to move from side to side. In this way, phony bills are spotted easily.

During most of the twentieth century—from 1929 to the 1990s—U.S. currency stayed the same without any major changes. Recently, however, the government has tried to redesign U.S. currency every seven to ten years to stay ahead of the counterfeiters. In the mid-1990s images on U.S. bills were enlarged as the first security measure. Starting in 2003, splashes of color have been added to the $20 bill and other currencies in order to make them more difficult to counterfeit.

"Counterfeiting is becoming highly organized and highly efficient," says Larry Felix, director of the Bureau of Engraving and Printing. "Currency is essentially a confidence situation. You have to always stay ahead in changes."

QUESTIONS TO CONSIDER:

■ Have you ever seen a counterfeit bill? How were you able to distinguish it from a real one? Name some other valuable items that people try to copy. Think of some ways you would be able to tell the copy from the authentic item.

■ Ideas are also counterfeited. Sometimes people try to give us false messages about who we are and how we should live our lives. What are some of those false messages? How can we distinguish counterfeit ideas from truth?

■ There is no way to put a security thread on an idea! We need a way to distinguish true messages from false ones. This is especially true when we try to distinguish between Christianity and "false gospels." The Bible points out three specific differences between a true message about God and a false message. Let's see what they are.

Copyright © 2009 Standard Publishing. All rights reserved. Permission to photocopy for ministry purposes only—not for resale.

BIBLE TRUTHS

from what they witnessed firsthand (1 John 1:1). Unlike religions, Christianity's source is God's truth, not human opinion. Destructive cults start when a leader begins claiming that his personal opinions are revelations from God.

BIBLE**TRUTH** 1

God frees us; religion enslaves us. GALATIANS 1:6, 7

■ **What do you know about other world religions? What is more important to them, law or grace?**

INSIDE STORY: As the gospel message penetrated the Gentile world, controversies began to stir regarding the role of the law of Moses in the Christian's life. Paul understood that God's good news was that people are saved by grace, not works (Ephesians 2:8, 9). This brought Paul into sharp conflict with a group of Christians known as Judaizers who taught that Gentiles needed to become Jews to become Christians (Acts 15:5). Paul retorted that the message preached by the Judaizers was really not good news (Galatians 1:7). Paul pointed out the hypocrisy of demanding that the Gentiles keep the law when Jews had never been able to do so (Romans 2:17-24), a statement to which Peter agreed (Acts 15:10).

BIBLE**TRUTH** 2

God reveals his truth; religion enforces opinion.
GALATIANS 1:8-12

■ **Think of someone whose personality or intellect makes whatever he says convincing. What is the danger of that?**

INSIDE STORY: In Paul's day, Jews not only studied the law of Moses, but the traditional teachings about the law as well. When Jewish priests became Christians (Acts 6:7), this practice came with them. Perhaps it was some of these learned priests who opposed Paul. Paul said that it didn't matter who taught salvation by works, even if it were an angel (Galatians 1:8)! What was important was whether teaching was truly from God. Paul explained that the good news he taught was given to him directly from Jesus (vv. 11, 12). Peter would later write that prophecy does not come from human wisdom but from the Holy Spirit (2 Peter 1:21). The apostle John made it clear that the message that he and other apostles taught came not from what they thought, but

BIBLE**TRUTH** 3

God changes our nature; religion controls our actions. GALATIANS 1:13-24

■ **How long can you be good? A week? A day? An hour? Why do we inevitably fail when we try to control our actions?**

INSIDE STORY: Because Jews had the law of Moses, their standard of morality was much higher than the Greek world's (Galatians 2:15). It might have appeared quite logical to try to get Gentiles to accept Jewish cultural norms before allowing them to be Christians. There was only one problem with that. Jews were sinners too! In fact, Paul, though a zealous keeper of the Jewish law, persecuted the church (Galatians 1:13). Though a good Jew, Paul admitted that he was the worst of all sinners (1 Timothy 1:12-16). It was not law keeping that changed Paul. It was a new life in Christ granted by grace.

Religion would rather control people's mode of dress or outward lifestyle than allow real alteration of life. Throughout the centuries believers tried to mark themselves with tonsures (special haircuts) or distinctive apparel. Dressing up a sinner is merely an attempt to control. Only Christ can bring real change.

CHALLENGE

Write these statements on the board: I still think of my faith in terms of rules to follow rather than as a relationship with Jesus. I will memorize John 8:31, 32; I tend to learn about God from what others say about him rather than by reading the Bible myself. I will memorize Acts 17:11; My Christian walk is more of a surface matter than a deep-down purity. I will memorize Psalm 51:2, 10. Read these Scriptures and encourage students to memorize one that speaks to them.

Copyright © 2009 Standard Publishing. All rights reserved. Permission to photocopy for ministry purposes only—not for resale.

Dare I Be Honest with God?

THE BIG TRUTH

CONFIDENTIAL SOURCE:
GALATIANS 2:9-16

PRETENDING WE ARE SOMEONE WE ARE NOT THREATENS ALL OF OUR RELATIONSHIPS.

At Any Cost

What values would someone compromise for money and fame? In the case of a TV reality show a few years ago, both parents and producers seemed to be willing to turn their backs on their responsibilities toward others in order to achieve commercial success.

The premise of *Kid Nation* was that forty minors, ages eight to fifteen, would live in a New Mexico ghost town for forty days to form their own community without parents. Show creator Tom Forman quipped that he wanted "kids to succeed where adults have failed." But before the show aired, news outlets uncovered some dangerous incidents that allegedly occurred during filming.

The *New York Times* reported that a couple of young people "required medical attention after drinking bleach that had been left in an unmarked soda bottle, according to both a parent and CBS. One eleven-year-old girl burned her face with splattered grease while cooking." *Television Week* said that the New Mexico Department of Labor claimed the children worked up to fourteen hours a day. But CBS contradicted that claim by saying this show didn't require the kids to "work" and that they were not CBS employees. A couple of parents of the participants explained that the experience was more like camp. The New Mexico attorney general investigated to see if any child labor laws were broken.

The *L.A. Times* interviewed four of the participants from the show, who said they "had to rough it without electricity or running water, sleep on bed rolls on the floor, cook their own meals, clean the town, run businesses, survive on three changes of clothes and set up their own hours and rules. . . . All four said the most challenging aspect was getting used to being filmed constantly."

Kids were paid a $5,000 stipend and could win rewards, including the grand prize of $20,000. In order to participate, the parents had to sign a contract with the following terms: "I understand that the Program may take place in inherently dangerous travel areas that may expose the Minor and other participants to a variety of unmarked and uncontrolled hazards and conditions that may cause the Minor serious bodily injury, illness or death . . ." (Reported by *Entertainment Weekly*.)

"Who is ultimately responsible here, the network that dangles the $20,000 prize in front of these parents or the parents who have allowed or encouraged their children to move forward with this situation?" asked Matthew Smith, chairman of the Department of Communication at Wittenberg University in Ohio and editor of "Survivor Lessons: Essays on Communication and Reality Television."

QUESTIONS TO CONSIDER:

■ Do you think a parent should allow a child to go on a show if he or she had to sign a contract that included the terms from the article above? Why or why not? What benefits could be gained were a child to go on a show like this? What risks are involved?

■ Whether we agree or disagree with the parents who let their children be on Kid Nation, some critics called them hypocrites because they let their kids take such risks. Some say CBS was being hypocritical because they made money at the expense of children's safety. How do you define *hypocrisy*?

■ Hypocrisy is not a new trend. For as long as humans have existed, we have been tempted to say one thing but do another. Let's look at the negative results that can come from hypocritical actions.

INSTANT STUDY 32 ■ NEW TESTAMENT

Copyright © 2009 Standard Publishing. All rights reserved. Permission to photocopy for ministry purposes only—not for resale.

BIBLE**TRUTH** 1

Hypocrisy causes us to break our promises.
GALATIANS 2:9-12

■ **Tell about a time when it was really hard to do the right thing. What made it so difficult?**

INSIDE STORY: Shortly after his conversion, the Lord spoke to Paul, assigning him the mission of bringing the gospel to Gentiles (Acts 22:21). Afterwards, Paul and Barnabas both met with James (the son of Mary and Joseph) and the apostles Peter and John, who affirmed their support for that mission (Galatians 2:9). But when Peter later visited Antioch, he seemed to withdraw his promise to support Gentile Christians. When some Judaizers came to Antioch, Peter shunned Gentile Christians. Since meals were mentioned, it seems that Peter was treating believers that God had cleansed with the blood of Jesus as ceremonially unclean (vv. 11, 12). This was not only a violation of the promise made to Paul and Barnabas; it was also a violation of a command God himself had given Peter earlier (Acts 10:15).

American politics teem with examples of how hypocrisy leads to broken promises. While running for president in 1988, George H. W. Bush promised, "Read my lips; no new taxes." After he was elected, however, he signed a tax increase into law. In 1992, Bill Clinton promised, if elected, to lead the most moral administration in American history. His eight years in office, ironically, will be remembered for unprecedented scandal. Hypocrisy leads to broken promises.

BIBLE**TRUTH** 2

Hypocrisy causes us to lead others astray.
GALATIANS 2:13

■ **Name a Christian leader you admire. How would it affect you if that person renounced his or her faith? Why?**

INSIDE STORY: Peter was so intimidated by the emissaries sent by James that he gradually withdrew from the Gentiles to avoid criticism (v. 12). This was a move motivated by fear, not truth. Notice the domino effect of hypocrisy. The Jewish believers of Antioch, following Peter's lead, withdrew from their Gentile Christian brethren. This introduced legalism into the church and split the fellowship. Apparently, the Jewish Christians adopted the legalism of the Judaizers and brought such pressure upon Barnabas that he joined in their withdrawal. It is interesting to note when Barnabas was first sent to Antioch, he was described as "a good man, full of the Holy Spirit and faith" (Acts 11:24). Hypocrisy can have a powerful impact on the best of people.

BIBLE**TRUTH** 3

Hypocrisy causes us to abandon our principles.
GALATIANS 2:14-16

■ **Who in your life would confront you if you were about to make a serious mistake? How do you feel about that?**

INSIDE STORY: The serious consequences of Peter's public sin demanded a public rebuke (v. 14). Paul told Peter that he was turning his back on what he knew to be true, the core gospel message (vv. 15, 16). Paul knew that Peter had earlier obeyed God's command to preach to Cornelius, a Gentile. At that time, Peter had defended his action by saying that to turn his back on Gentiles would have been to oppose God (Acts 11:17). Now, because of a hypocrisy born of fear, Peter had turned his back on the beliefs he once expressed. It is one thing to preach a belief. It is another to practice that belief when times get tough. Accountability to other believers is the answer.

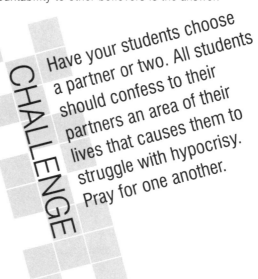

CHALLENGE

Have your students choose a partner or two. All students should confess to their partners an area of their lives that causes them to struggle with hypocrisy. Pray for one another.

Copyright © 2009 Standard Publishing. All rights reserved. Permission to photocopy for ministry purposes only—not for resale.

THE **BIG** TRUTH

OUR HEAVENLY FATHER IS A LOVING DADDY.

CONFIDENTIAL SOURCE:
GALATIANS 3:23-4:7

Am I a Slave or a Son?

Certainly Uncertain

The war in Iraq has caused uncertainty in the minds of the American people. This has been true of people in every strata of American life.

In the fall of 2007, General David Petraeus (Pe-TRAY-us) went before Congress to deliver a long-awaited assessment of Iraq and the troop surge. Even before he took the floor, Patraeus was the target of harsh words from anti-war groups. The left-wing political action committee, MoveOn.Org, paid for newspaper ads attacking the integrity of the general. Patraeus was accused of "cooking the books for the White House" and was labeled "General Betray-us," using wordplay on his name.

As Petraeus entered the Congressional hearing anti-war protesters taunted him, shouting, "Tell the truth, general." During the hearing itself, a heckler interrupted the session, trying to keep the general from speaking. Patraeus did not respond in kind to the protestors or the heckler, who was quickly removed from the hearing room.

Democrats were kind to the general but still strongly opposed the war. They strongly opposed the surge in troops eight months earlier, when President Bush announced the increase in the number of American troops deployed in the Iraq War to provide security to Baghdad and Al Anbar Province. At that time, critics predicted failure of the troop increase, a growth in violence, and even war with Iran. Now that the surge had proven successful in quelling violence and none of the dire predictions had occurred, critics argued that the Iraqi government was not making sufficient political process. Representative Tom Lantos, a Democrat from California said, "Military progress without political progress is meaningless."

The Republicans were quick to fire back at their political rivals. Representative Duncan Hunter of California, the first Republican to speak at the hearing, criticized Democrats for having made up their minds in advance of the nationally televised hearing. Responding to anti-war ads and protests, Senator Mitch McConnell of Kentucky admonished, "These childish tactics are an insult to everyone fighting for our freedom in Iraq, and they should be condemned."

QUESTIONS TO CONSIDER:

■ What do you remember about the Iraq discussion at that time? Had the debate increased your understanding, or did it simply add to your uncertainty about how the conflict should be handled? Explain. What would it have taken for you to feel less uncertain and more confident about the final outcome of the war?

■ What are some other conditions in your life and in our world today that make you feel uncomfortable and uncertain? Why do you feel that way? What would it take to ease your apprehensions?

■ The world is full of uncertainties. We may wonder what will happen as a result of war, injustice, pollution, and a host of other problems. On the other hand, God tells us that we have reasons for confidence despite uncertainties. Let's look at three certainties we enjoy as children of God.

INSTANT**STUDY 33** ■ NEW**TESTAMENT**

71

Copyright © 2009 Standard Publishing. All rights reserved. Permission to photocopy for ministry purposes only—not for resale.

BIBLE**TRUTH** 1

When God is our Father, we are free from legalism. GALATIANS 3:23-25; 4:1-5

■ **What household chores do you perform? Why do you think that you are required to do those chores?**

INSIDE STORY: When a child refuses to do his or her household chores, parents might withhold allowance or privileges. But if parents had hired a servant to do this same job and had these results, they would have fired the hired hand long ago! A child may be disciplined, but he or she does not have to worry about being removed from the family!

Paul explained the purpose of the law to the Galatians (3:23). A child of a billionaire is born an heir of the family fortune, but a checkbook isn't presented at birth! Rather, that heir has tutors who teach the maturing child what a responsible heir looks like (4:2). That tutoring does not earn inheritance, but prepares one to handle it. Likewise, the law does not earn salvation, but leads us to accept the grace of God in Christ (3:24).

As a child of God we are loved because of that relationship, not judged by our job performance! We are freed from the fear that God is looking for reasons to kick us out of his family when we sin.

BIBLE**TRUTH** 2

When God is our Father, we are united with all others who are his children. GALATIANS 3:26-28

■ **It has been said, "You can pick your friends, but you are stuck with family." What does that mean to you?**

INSIDE STORY: People in Paul's day could recognize the children of an earthly king by their royal robes. Paul pointed out to the Galatians that they could be certain that they were God's children because those that had been baptized into Christ had been clothed with Christ (v. 27). Christians are related because we share the same Holy Spirit who lives within us from the time of our conversion (Acts 2:38). That

Spirit alters our behavior, giving us a family resemblance that we share with others in the family of God. When God is our Father, we have a wonderfully diverse group of brothers and sisters—Jews and Greeks, free people and slaves, and men and women (Galatians 3:28). When we are dressed in the robe of Christ, we are part of a royal household that includes those "from every tribe and language and people and nation" (Revelation 5:9).

BIBLE**TRUTH** 3

When God is our Father, we share God's riches for eternity. GALATIANS 3:29; 4:6, 7

■ **How would your life change if it were discovered that you were the child of a billionaire? How would that be proven?**

INSIDE STORY: Children of the king do not only have the privilege of living like royalty now. We will inherit the wealth of the entire kingdom! Abraham was declared righteous because of his faith (Romans 4). He received God's covenant promise that he would be the ancestor of a great nation that would bring God's blessings to the entire world (Genesis 12:2, 3; 28:14). This promise was also given to Abraham's seed, Jesus Christ (Galatians 3:16; Acts 3:25). If we are in Christ because of our faith, then we are Abraham's spiritual seed also. This means we are the heirs of the spiritual blessings God promised Abraham. What if someone claims to be the long-lost child of a billionaire today? Modern science can determine whether someone is related to someone else by DNA testing. Paul said that we know we are the heirs of God's kingdom because we share the same spiritual DNA. "God sent the Spirit of his Son into our hearts" (Galatians 4:6).

CHALLENGE Have your students use paper and markers to create Heavenly Father's Day cards. These cards should express reasons why we are thankful that God is our father.

Copyright © 2009 Standard Publishing. All rights reserved. Permission to photocopy for ministry purposes only—not for resale.

What Gives Me Direction?

Our Guiding Document

September 17 is a holiday. How do you celebrate it? Were you even aware of its existence? A study shows that most teens know little about Constitution Day.

The United States Constitution was signed on September 17, 1787. Congress created Constitution Day in 2004 and requires any school or college receiving federal money to teach about the Constitution on or around September 17. Schools can decide for themselves how they celebrate the day, but each school must have a Constitution Day educational program every year.

At Lawler Elementary in Kentucky, every student wore a red, white, and blue T-shirt, gathered around the flagpole, and sang patriotic songs such as "America the Beautiful" and "This Land is Your Land." Students at Eastern New Mexico University in Roswell honored veterans of Walker Air Force Base at a Constitution Day reception. Boston University handed out Constitution Day bookmarks and hosted a lecture on the First Amendment. Wittenberg University in Springfield, Ohio, distributed pocket copies of the Constitution and served patriotic meals colored in red, white, and blue in the school cafeteria.

Just one in ten students could remember how his or her high school celebrated Constitution Day last year, according to a study paid for by the John S. and James L. Knight Foundation in Miami. Eric Newton, vice president of the foundation's journalism program, said he worries that an entire generation may lack a solid understanding of the document that is the final authority of our government.

Senator Robert Byrd was responsible for the creation Constitution Day. The senator from West Virginia always carries a copy of the Constitution in his pocket as a way to ensure that proposed laws are in keeping with the law of the land. "I refer to it and study its provisions every day," claims Byrd. He further warns, "Without constant study and renewal of our knowledge of the Constitution and its history we are in peril of allowing our freedoms to erode. . . . [You cannot] forget your responsibilities as a citizen to monitor the government leaders you have elected and see to it that they defend and uphold the Constitution."

QUESTIONS TO CONSIDER:

■ How did your school celebrate Constitution Day this year? How important is this day to you? Why do you view it this way?

■ Explain why Senator Byrd carries a copy of the U.S. Constitution in his pocket. Why do you think that this practice is appropriate for someone who has to distinguish between good and bad proposed laws in his job? Think of tools you may use to determine truth. For example, how do you check to see if a word is spelled correctly, a calculation or measurement is correct, or that a claim someone makes can be supported? Why are such tools necessary?

■ We all recognize that we must distinguish truth from falsehood everyday. Something in human nature always seems to be trying to deceive and manipulate. But God tells us that there is a way we can have life qualities that are real and not counterfeit. Let's contrast the characteristics of human nature and godly nature.

INSTANT **STUDY 34** ■ **NEW TESTAMENT**

Copyright © 2009 Standard Publishing. All rights reserved. Permission to photocopy for ministry purposes only—not for resale.

BIBLE TRUTHS

BIBLE**TRUTH** 1

Human nature leads us to rebel against God.
GALATIANS 5:17, 19-21

■ **What does evil mean to you? Where does it come from? What does it look like?**

INSIDE STORY: Raging inside each of us is a war between the sinful nature and the Holy Spirit (Galatians 5:16, 17). The sinful nature produces evil character traits. They reflect the sin of Adam and Eve who sought to be like God, thereby distancing them from him. Those works of the flesh fall into three general categories.

We seek to satisfy the appetites of our bodies. The first three acts cover all sexual offenses (v. 19). "Immorality" is the broadest term referring to any inappropriate sexual behavior. "Impurity" speaks of a filthiness of heart and mind that makes a person unclean. "Debauchery" refers to the act of satisfying any and all sensual desires out of habit without shame.

We reject the one true God and look for less demanding substitutes. Spiritual infidelity is the focus of the second category (v. 20). "Idolatry" refers to the worship of created things as opposed to worship of the creator. In today's culture, the influence of "witchcraft" is seen in tarot cards, horoscopes, psychics, Wicca, and other elevated-consciousness philosophies.

We use people, destroying healthy relationships with each other. Paul's third category comprises a series of social sins that destroy personal relationships in three different ways. "Hatred, discord, jealousy, fits of rage" (v. 20) show aggression. Acts of violence and threats to person and property are declarations of interpersonal war. "Selfish ambition, dissensions, factions and envy" (vv. 20, 21) destroy relationships by breaking people into opposing camps. It becomes "us" against "them." Finally, "drunkenness, orgies, and the like" (v. 21) turn the individual into the supreme being of his or her own world. Personal needs are placed above the needs of others.

BIBLE**TRUTH** 2

The Holy Spirit can shape our spirits so that we comply with God's nature. GALATIANS 5:16, 18, 22-26

■ **List physical traits you get from your parents. What traits do you think you would inherit as a child of God?**

INSIDE STORY: When the Spirit controls our daily walk, he produces fruit that can be divided into three general categories:

God occupies the center of life. "Love, joy, peace" (v. 22) are the result of having a right relationship with God. When we grasp the sacrificial love of God in Christ, we are willing to give up the priceless to someone regardless of his or her attractiveness or worthiness. Peace is the rest we enjoy when we know that God is in control of our lives and not we ourselves. Joy is knowing that God's long-term plan for us is for good.

Others are viewed as more important than ourselves. The next three attributes, found in verse 22, describe our relationships with other people. "Patience" comes from the Greek words for great anger. It is the surrender of our right to act upon great and legitimate anger. "Kindness" literally means allowing ourselves to be used. Human nature seeks to use others. The Holy Spirit allows us to surrender ourselves to others. "Goodness" means that we behave toward others in a morally perfect way. It is asking, "What would Jesus do?"

We become more like Christ. Christian maturity is the focus of the final three virtues. Though it seems unusual to us, the English words faith and "faithfulness"(v. 22) are the same word in Greek. A faithful person has faith that God will act righteously and inspires that same faith in others. "Gentleness" (v. 23) is not weakness, but great strength that is used to serve rather than dominate others. We have "self-control" (v. 23) when we show the ability to force our will to overcome the desires of our body, even when those desires may seem logical to our minds. These final three virtues cause us to more fully reflect the nature of Jesus.

CHALLENGE

Close with a fruit feast. Review the attributes the Spirit wants to plant in our lives while snacking on a variety of fresh fruit together.

Copyright © 2009 Standard Publishing. All rights reserved. Permission to photocopy for ministry purposes only—not for resale.

What's So Great About the Church?

A Little Help from His Friends

Though celebrations differ, teens throughout the world commemorate "coming of age." Whether with the coming out ball of high society debutantes, the *Quinceañera* (the fifteenth birthday party for girls in Spanish-speaking communities), or the sweet sixteen party, we recognize that the passage into adulthood brings an increase of power, privileges, and authority. One California teen, however, made his entrance into adulthood a time of partnership rather than of privilege.

Culver City High School student Saleem Thompson decided to host his sixteenth birthday bash and do something different. Saleem invited friends, teachers, parents, and teens all across Los Angeles to come out, celebrate life, and work as a team to give to the neediest people in the community. In sharp contrast to MTV's *My Super Sweet Sixteen*, which chronicles the excesses of selfish teenagers, Saleem's party was called "16, Cool, and Giving Back."

Saleem intended to make his peers more aware of the homeless in Los Angeles, to have his classmates and local teens from surrounding high schools donate to the Los Angeles Homeless Services Coalition, and to sponsor a team effort that would make a difference in his southern California community. Held at the famous Hollywood House of Blues, "16, Cool, and Giving Back" was a fundraiser *for* teens organized *by* teens.

The party gained national attention as the day approached. Celebrities made guest appearances. Corporations donated food and merchandise for games and contests. And each of the nearly five hundred attendees that walked across the red carpet to enter the celebration found a "cool can" into which he or she was able to place a personal donation.

Giving back is nothing new for Saleem. It started when he was five and was ready to enter kindergarten. Then and every year since, he and his mother would go through his closet and donate his old clothes to local charities. After doing some research on local charities, Saleem was shocked to learn that there are over ninety thousand homeless adults and teens in the Los Angeles area. He hopes that he and fellow teens can continue to do something about that problem.

QUESTIONS TO CONSIDER:

■ Sometimes we look at big problems in the world and feel that one person can do nothing about them. How did Saleem recruit partners and create a spirit of teamwork to do what one person alone could not do? How might this approach be used to solve some problems in your community?

■ Think of times in your life when you joined with others to accomplish something. What did you do? How did working with partners make a job easier to accomplish than if the same number of people were just working on their own?

■ When we become Christians, we join a team. The church is a community of partners, working together to accomplish big things in the lives of one another and in our neighborhoods. God tells us some characteristics of the teamwork we have as being a part of the church. Let's discover how that teamwork can change us and others.

INSTANT **STUDY** 35 ■ NEW **TESTAMENT**

75

Copyright © 2009 Standard Publishing. All rights reserved. Permission to photocopy for ministry purposes only—not for resale.

BIBLE TRUTHS

In a healthy Christian community, no one believes that he or she has all the answers. Peter observed that we all need to "grow up" in our salvation (1 Peter 2:2). Furthermore we all need to show gratitude to mature Christians who teach us (Galatians 6:6; 1 Timothy 5:17, 18; Hebrews 13:7).

BIBLE**TRUTH** 1

Members of the Christian community aid one another when they struggle. GALATIANS 6:1, 2

■ **What are some ways people react when they see someone hurting? How do you think they should react? What keeps them from doing so?**

INSIDE STORY: When Christians struggle, their brothers and sisters in Christ may turn against them. Paul told the Galatians that Christians must work at gently restoring the sinning believer (v. 1). We see an example of this in the church at Corinth. A man in that congregation committed the repulsive sin of having a sexual relationship with his stepmother! Because he was unrepentant, Paul told the church to exclude him from fellowship (1 Corinthians 5:1, 2, 13). This discipline caused the man to repent. Paul then told the church to "comfort him" and "reaffirm [their] love for him" (2 Corinthians 2:5-8).

When the church becomes a hospital for sinners rather than a vacation resort for saints, we "will fulfill the law of Christ" (Galatians 6:2). "A new command I give you: Love one another. As I have loved you, so you must love one another. By this all men will know that you are my disciples, if you love one another" (John 13:34, 35).

BIBLE**TRUTH** 2

Members of the Christian community recognize that they still have much to learn. GALATIANS 6:3-6

■ **Is there a right way or a wrong way to correct someone? Give examples.**

INSIDE STORY: In a memorable scene from the film *Malice* (1993), the arrogant Dr. Jed Hill boasted, "You ask me if I have a God complex. Let me tell you something: I *am* God." This caricature of an arrogant doctor rings true. Those who correct problems of others may get haughty.

BIBLE**TRUTH** 3

Members of the Christian community await the day when salvation is complete. GALATIANS 6:7-10

■ **What do you think it is like to live without hope? How does having hope make a difference?**

INSIDE STORY: It is easy to look at the trouble in the world and question God's justice. But disciples of Jesus are called to encourage each other to hold on and to spur one another on to good deeds (Hebrews 10:23-25). The one who plants evil will ultimately be destroyed, and the one who "sows to please the Spirit" will be rewarded eternally (Galatians 6:7, 8).

This is why we must "not give up" and keep doing "good to all people" (vv. 9, 10).

CHALLENGE Take some time to brainstorm a way your students can encourage fellow believers in the next month (e.g., fold bulletins, go calling with the ministers, take food to the sick, work in the nursery, clean the church, etc.).

Copyright © 2009 Standard Publishing. All rights reserved. Permission to photocopy for ministry purposes only—not for resale.

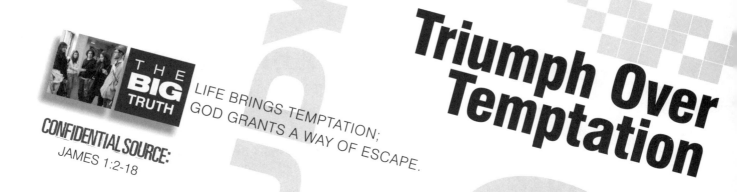

Triumph Over Temptation

Tricked into Being Good

Overcoming temptation of any kind requires discipline, self-control, and other hard-to-practice qualities. But what if there were a shortcut? What if psychologists could alter your thought process and make you stop desiring the tempting item you crave? This possibility is getting closer to becoming a reality.

The concept of false memories was publicized a few years ago when a panel of psychologists proved that thoughts and ideas could be placed in people's heads to make them believe things actually happened. The study was being done to see if questioning by psychologists and police officers during investigations were actually planting ideas in people's heads instead of bringing up factual information.

Dr. Elizabeth F. Loftus, a professor of psychology and criminology at the University of California at Irvine, described a study of 20,000 volunteers. A third of the participants said they remember being hugged by Bugs Bunny at Disneyland when they were children. (You may realize this has to be false because Bugs Bunny is from Warner Brothers, not Disney.) Researchers had planted this false memory in the volunteers' minds, but the participants felt the emotions as if the experiences were real.

Additionally, Dr. Loftus and her team have discovered that food memories are very easy to manipulate. So they studied 336 college students. The students were asked about some memories they had about food as children. A week later, a false memory was planted among their true memories. The false one made the students think they had gotten sick after eating pickles and eggs when they were children. Later all the students were interviewed about foods they would likely eat if offered to them. Now 40 percent said they would avoid pickles and eggs because those foods made them sick. Another study made people believe that they liked the taste of asparagus.

Whether these new "memories" will permanently affect behavior remains to be seen. "What we'd like to do now," said Dr. Loftus, "is take the students out for a real picnic and see what happens."

QUESTIONS
TO CONSIDER:

■ Name some foods you remember loving as a child. Name some foods you remember hating as a child. If your food memories could be changed, what food would you want to avoid? What food would you choose to crave?

■ What do you think about this idea of manipulating memories? If you could alter your mind in order to avoid temptation, would you do it? Why or why not? Do you think mind alteration could make people avoid temptation completely, or would new temptations always pop up? Defend your answer.

■ We are told in the Bible that we will always face temptations because we are sinful human beings. That would mean that no amount of memory alteration could keep us from being tempted. But there is hope! We can seek a spiritual alteration to help us resist temptation. In the Bible, James reveals four sources of temptations. Let's find out what they are and how we can resist them.

INSTANT **STUDY 36** ■ **NEW TESTAMENT**

Copyright © 2009 Standard Publishing. All rights reserved. Permission to photocopy for ministry purposes only—not for resale.

BIBLE TRUTHS

BIBLE**TRUTH** 1

The struggles of life can create opportunities for temptation. JAMES 1:2-4

■ **Tell about a time when you were totally discouraged. How did that situation affect your behavior?**

INSIDE STORY: The first kind of trial occurs when tough times discourage us and tempt us to give up following God. James's prescription for overcoming this temptation is to "tough it out." When we do so, we will grow closer to spiritual maturity. That maturity finally is complete when we receive the eternal crown of life God has promised.

Harriet Tubman was born into slavery, yet she allowed her suffering to create a compassion for others who suffered. Though she had escaped the country, Harriet Tubman returned to the area in which she had been enslaved and helped lead three hundred others to freedom in the movement known as the Underground Railroad.

BIBLE**TRUTH** 2

Our lack of wisdom can allow us to stumble into temptation. JAMES 1:5-8

■ **Tell about a time you did something wrong purely out of ignorance. Did you ever make that mistake again?**

INSIDE STORY: A second problem occurs when our lack of spiritual wisdom leads us to be unstable and uncertain about what we should do. We can ask God and he will generously give us wisdom. God's inspired Word is a totally reliable source of that wisdom in practical, everyday situations (2 Timothy 3:16, 17).

Dottie had always been taught that she should find her handsome prince, get married, and live happily ever after. But her fairy-tale marriage did not bring the love she desired. After attending a church retreat with her husband, they both learned that it was God, not each other, who needed to be first in their lives.

BIBLE**TRUTH** 3

Being poor can present temptations to us. JAMES 1:9-11

■ **How much money is enough, in your opinion? Do you think everyone who has that much is satisfied? Explain.**

INSIDE STORY: The third source of temptation is our possessions. When we believe we do not have enough, we are led into envy and even violence (James 4:1-5). When we have plenty, we are tempted to be arrogant and seek security in those possessions. James tells us that we must learn to be content in whatever financial state we find ourselves.

BIBLE **TRUTH** 4

The urges of our fallen nature can draw us into temptation. JAMES 1:12-18

■ **If you know what is right, will you do it every time? Why or why not?**

INSIDE STORY: The fourth source of temptation is our own fallen nature. James warns us not to blame God for our desires. God does not give people temptations (James 1:13); all his gifts are good (v. 17). The temptations we face come from within. But these temptations are still deceptive and deadly. Like fish lured out of hiding we are dragged away; like animals attracted to the bait in a trap we are enticed. Our own appetites and desires, if left uncontrolled, eventually give birth to sin. Then sin, when it reaches its conclusion, gives birth to death.

CHALLENGE Distribute a Chinese finger puzzle to each student. These toys tighten their grip the harder you try to pull away. Have students keep them as a reminder to flee temptation God's way, not their way.

Copyright © 2009 Standard Publishing. All rights reserved. Permission to photocopy for ministry purposes only—not for resale.

Fight Favoritism

Seeing Red

What do you feel about the color purple? Is it more soothing and less frightening than red? Many teachers think so. A new trend is emerging among educators—they are putting down their red pens and choosing different colors to mark on students' papers.

"If you see a whole paper of red, it looks pretty frightening," said Sharon Carlson, a middle school health and physical education teacher in Massachusetts. "Purple stands out, but it doesn't look as scary as red."

Other teachers agree with the color switch. "It's just too harsh," said Debbie Levin, an eighth grade teacher in Georgia. "I will use purple or green, but never red. I think it's very demoralizing for a child to have written a creative paper and to have it marked up all in red to show that it's awful."

"Red has a negative connotation, and we want to promote self-confidence," said Robin Slipakoff, a second and third grade teacher in Florida.

Red ink usage began in the 1700s when clerks and accountants dipped their quills in red to indicate mistakes. From there, teachers adopted the practice. But some teachers say it doesn't matter if seeing red raises students' blood pressure a little. That's the point!

"I want it to be visually startling to the student and say to that student, 'I didn't do my best work here,'" said Carol Jago, a high school English teacher in California who has been using a red pen for her thirty-one years of teaching. She compares the ink with the red of a stop sign—placed there to point out a dangerous problem. "I want to hurt their feelings a little bit," said Jago. But before you think she's just out to inflict pain on students, read Jago's motivation:

"Red is honest, direct, and to the point. I'm sending the message, 'I care about you enough to care how you present yourself to the outside world.'"

For now, the debate continues. But ink companies are making sure they are prepared. The next time you're in a store that sells school supplies, check out the amount of purple pens they have in stock!

QUESTIONS TO CONSIDER:

■ How do you feel when you see the color red? Would you care if your teachers changed their ink color? Which means more—the color of the ink or the words the teacher writes? Do you agree with the people who said red ink causes emotional distress or with the people who said red is OK because it draws attention to the problems? Explain your answers.

■ Does it matter if all teachers agree on their color of ink? Why or why not? What is your favorite color of ink to write with and why?

■ Is there a difference between having favorite things and showing favoritism toward people? Defend your answer.

■ We all have favorite things—favorite clothing, favorite music, and even favorite colors of ink pens! But having favorite people is a different matter altogether. Prejudice, discrimination, and bigotry cause damage to the church of Jesus Christ. James tells us there are three negative results of favoritism. Let's read about those now.

Copyright © 2009 Standard Publishing. All rights reserved. Permission to photocopy for ministry purposes only—not for resale.

BIBLE TRUTHS

BIBLE**TRUTH** 1

Favoritism causes us to overlook people God considers to be valuable. JAMES 2:1-4

■ **When have you felt excluded or snubbed? Why do you think you were excluded? Why was that not a good reason?**

INSIDE STORY: James squarely confronted the favoritism issue with a hypothetical situation. Suppose they were in their regular meeting place (usually in a private home), and a rich man entered. They would notice him and offer him the best chair. When an obviously poor man entered, the Christians let him sit on the floor! To the material world, this would make sense. If you are going to have a "church club," why not restrict it to people who could add to your treasury? Why should we allow people in who will drain our resources rather than add to them?

Compare James 2:5 to Luke 6:20. James seems to be paraphrasing the words of his half-brother, Jesus. Both probably recalled the words of Moses, who warned Israel that those who had plenty would tend to "forget the LORD your God, who brought you out of Egypt" (Deuteronomy 8:10-14). The church is richer when it has poor people in it! From the poor, we see more clearly what dependence upon God looks like.

BIBLE**TRUTH** 2

Favoritism causes us to favor those who would do us harm. JAMES 2:5-7

■ **Sometimes we are drawn to the wrong crowd of people. Why do you think that might happen?**

INSIDE STORY: Groucho Marx is credited with saying, "I refuse to join any club that would have me as a member." We like people who are better than ourselves. We may find ourselves in such a group only to discover that we have to pretend that we are someone we are not in order to avoid expulsion! If James's readers were to make the right judgment

about "whose club to join," they needed to review the facts. Who were the ones who had become rich by exploiting the poor (v. 6) and not paying them fair wages? (See James 5:4.) Who had become rich by dragging people into court and suing them? Who were so arrogant in their riches that they blasphemed the Lord's name? If this was the way rich people got their money, and if this was the way they acted, why should Christians be in such a rush to honor them? When the church caters to those the world honors, we are in danger of welcoming those who would do us harm.

BIBLE**TRUTH** 3

Favoritism keeps us from becoming godlier.
JAMES 2:8, 9

■ **Complete this sentence: "Having _____ as a friend makes me a better person." Explain.**

INSIDE STORY: The cure for favoritism lies in what James calls "the royal law." It is found in the Old Testament (Leviticus 19:18). Jesus called it the second greatest commandment (Matthew 22:39). Paul said it summarized all of God's law for us (Galatians 5:14). The law of God's kingdom is, "Love your neighbor as yourself" (James 2:8). It will not do to love our neighbor and hate our enemy (Matthew 5:43), because this is discrimination. It will not do to exclude certain people from the neighbor list (Luke 10:29). The way Jesus explained it, our neighbor turns out to be everyone who is within the reach of our help. God loved us even when we were still his enemies, and we are expected to show the same kind of love to others (Romans 5:8-10). Furthermore, observable love for others within the church is the identifying mark of Christians for a watching world (John 13:34, 35).

CHALLENGE Help students to think like those whom they have offended. Ask them to think of someone they have shown favoritism against and to write a paragraph from that person's point of view explaining how he or she felt when that happened.

Copyright © 2009 Standard Publishing. All rights reserved. Permission to photocopy for ministry purposes only—not for resale.

Zip the Lip

It's How You Say It

Remember the hit song "Jesus Walks" by Kanye West? Hearing Jesus' name in mainstream music was surprising. Just as foreign might be hearing hip-hop music in the local church. But hip-hop could be on its way to a pew near you.

The world of the church and the world of hip-hop music are drawing closer together. Although the church has often feared this type of music, now many congregations are realizing that hip-hop music connects with younger generations and can be used for God's glory. This music is not a passing trend, and it doesn't have to always be about drugs, sex, and violence.

"Hip-hop is the language and the cry of this generation," said Adam Durso, a youth minister at a church in New York City. He leads a Friday night service that mixes preaching with guest rappers and videos. And some of these Christian rappers don't gloss over the hard stuff either. Their music reveals the artists' dark pasts yet how Jesus delivered them from their addictions.

Phil Jackson, a youth minister in the Chicago agrees with using hip-hop music. "For this generation, the only way to make the gospel relevant to them is through hip-hop. In my neighborhood we don't need another church on Sunday morning. We need something to speak to young people."

Others are approaching this evangelism technique in a different way. Youth minister Fred Lynch has produced an album called *The Epic*, translating the entire gospel of John into rap. A graphic novel accompanies the project. Augusta State University in Georgia hopes to show churches the need to move past their fears. "Mainline churches have identified hip-hop culture as an enemy, and that's their problem," Ralph Watkins, professor of African-American culture and religion, said. "If you walked in to 90 percent of your mainline churches who have not embraced this culture, you're going to find an absence of young people."

Perhaps Kanye West summed it up best himself. When Kanye's dad, a Christian marriage counselor, heard the song "Jesus Walks," he thought his son might have missed his calling to become a preacher. "I said, 'No, maybe this is my calling.'" Kanye described. "I reach more people than any one pastor can."

QUESTIONS TO CONSIDER:

■ Do you agree that hip-hop music has a big impact on people your age? What do you think about Kanye West's quote: "I reach more people than any one pastor can"? Is that true? Explain your answers. Would people you know be more likely to listen to the good news of Jesus if hip-hop music were involved? What other styles of music could be used to reach people your age for Jesus? Why are people affected by music? What power do song lyrics have?

■ Do words have power? Think about a time when you said something you regretted. Think about a time when someone's words made you feel terrific. Words can make you feel something. The right words encourage and empower. The wrong words can bring conflict and hatred. James warned of three dangers that come from uncontrolled speech. Let's look at them.

INSTANT**STUDY 38** ■ NEW**TESTAMENT**

Copyright © 2009 Standard Publishing. All rights reserved. Permission to photocopy for ministry purposes only—not for resale.

BIBLE TRUTHS

BIBLE**TRUTH** 1

When we do not control our speech, our whole life is out of control. JAMES 3:1-5A

■ **Tell about a time you formed of an opinion of someone based on the first words you heard that person speak.**

INSIDE STORY: Small things have big impacts. A small bit in a horse's mouth can turn the whole animal. A small rudder can turn a large ship. The tongue is not very big, but it is the steering wheel for our character. Solomon warned, "A fool's mouth is his undoing" (Proverbs 18:7). "Do not let your mouth lead you into sin" (Ecclesiastes 5:6). Jesus told the Pharisees that what they said was more important in shaping their lives than was the keeping of religious rituals (Matthew 15:11).

What subjects dominate our speech? A person always talking about money will probably be led into greed. A person always talking about sex might be led into impurity. A person using rough or violent language may soon become a rough, violent person. Our words can determine our direction.

BIBLE**TRUTH** 2

When we do not control our speech, we cause harm to ourselves and to those around us.
JAMES 3:5B-8

■ **How have you been hurt by the words of others? How were those words more damaging than if that person simply punched you?**

INSIDE STORY: Much of the tongue's potential is its ability to inflict damage. The tongue is like a spark near dry timber, an uncaged, dangerous animal, or a venomous snake (v. 5b-8). Uncontrolled words can bring devastating results.

Solomon spoke often of the destructive nature of uncontrolled words. "Violence overwhelms the mouth of the wicked" (Proverbs 10:6). Jesus told the Pharisees that they

were like poisonous snakes, a "brood of vipers," because their vicious words damaged their followers (Matthew 12:34). Countless lives have been altered by a few harsh words. Paul warned believers to make sure that we speak only helpful words, those "seasoned with salt," in order to build up and not destroy others (Colossians 4:6).

BIBLE**TRUTH** 3

When we do not control our speech, we fail to clearly reflect the nature of God. JAMES 3:9, 10

■ **Think of a Christian you admire. How would it affect your opinion of that person if you heard him or her using abusive language?**

INSIDE STORY: It is not enough to keep our tongues under control only part of the time. Those who wish to follow God must make sure that their words are consistent. The Jews of Ezekiel's day were condemned because "with their mouths they express[ed] devotion, but their hearts [were] greedy for unjust gain" (Ezekiel 33:31). Christians must rid themselves of "unwholesome talk" and take care that their words are "helpful for building others up according to their needs" (Ephesians 4:29). Our words should not show a divided body of Christ, but one with "a spirit of unity . . . so that with one heart and mouth [we] may glorify the God and Father of our Lord Jesus Christ" (Romans 15:5, 6). The world should expect to find a message from God in Christ's church. When we do not control our speech, we reflect an unclear image of God.

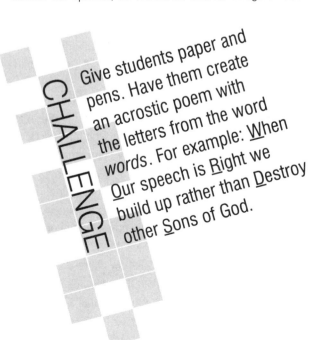

CHALLENGE

Give students paper and pens. Have them create an acrostic poem with the letters from the word words. For example: When Our speech is Right we build up rather than Destroy other Sons of God.

Copyright © 2009 Standard Publishing. All rights reserved. Permission to photocopy for ministry purposes only—not for resale.

THE BIG TRUTH

CONFIDENTIAL SOURCE:
JAMES 4:1-10

CHOOSING WHOM TO OBEY CAN
BRING FREEDOM OR SLAVERY.

Get a New Boss

The Way the Ball Bounces

The country of Sri Lanka had a perplexing mystery on its hands. The twenty-three-member national handball team of this Indian Ocean island nation vanished while competing in a tournament in Germany. One fact makes this disappearance even more puzzling: Sri Lanka *had* no national handball team.

Hemasiri Fernando, president of Sri Lanka's Olympic Association, said that while handball is popular in Europe, the sport has not caught on in his country. "There is no handball federation in Sri Lanka," stated Fernando. "We don't even have a single club."

Acting German Ambassador to Sri Lanka, Heidi Jung, reported that the so-called "team" managed to fool the German Embassy in Sri Lanka into issuing visas for a month-long tour. "They presented documents, and the documents looked all right," she said.

Political unrest has plagued Sri Lanka for years. The Tamils, the Hindu minority of Sri Lanka, have felt oppressed by the governing Buddhist majority of the nation. For the past number of years, thousands of Tamils have sought to escape their country and live in Europe. Since the late 1990s, European governments have usually rejected Tamil asylum seekers and returned them to Sri Lanka. It seems that these twenty-three men found a way to challenge the authorities of all of these nations and escape a government that they found to be oppressive.

Dietmer Doering, organizer of the tournament, recalled that the Sri Lankans were not doing well in the handball competition at the time of their disappearance. "We initially thought the team had gotten lost in nearby woods while jogging. We now know they crossed into Italy. They even left their dirty laundry."

"This will be the last time we will be doing this. I am not planning to invite any more teams from Sri Lanka," concluded Doering.

QUESTIONS
TO CONSIDER:

■ Describe the attitude this "handball team" displayed toward the authority of their nation and the authorities of other nations. Give a few examples from the article of that attitude.

■ Do you believe that deceiving authorities was OK to do in this situation? Is it OK to do all the time? Why or why not?

■ Name some authorities to which you have to submit. What is your attitude toward these authorities? Why do you hold such attitudes? Is it even necessary to have authority? Explain.

■ No doubt, all of us have some problem respecting authority. James recognizes that situation but also identifies the source of and solution to this attitude.

Copyright © 2009 Standard Publishing. All rights reserved. Permission to photocopy for ministry purposes only—not for resale.

BIBLE TRUTHS

BIBLE TRUTH 1

Our human nature leads us into constant conflict.
JAMES 4:1-3

■ **List things that make you angry. Try to determine the root cause of your anger.**

INSIDE STORY: Worldwide it is obvious from every newspaper headline. In our homes it is seen the first time a two-year-old stares into Mom's eyes and says, "No!" In our schools it is seen in the chaos that ensues when the teacher walks out of the classroom. On the street it is seen in gang violence. Humanity has an authority problem.

We must take personal responsibility for our desires, because they arise from within us—just like the lusts that give birth to sin (James 1:13-15). James emphasizes the nature of our problem by using three different terms—*desires*, *covet*, and *want*. We don't get what we want because we don't ask God, and when we do ask God we ask with the wrong motives. Like the prodigal son, we want to spend God's blessings on our pleasures.

BIBLE TRUTH 2

This conflict is caused by our rebellion against God's leadership. JAMES 4:4-6

■ **Tell about a time when someone you trusted betrayed you. Do you think God ever feels that way? Explain.**

INSIDE STORY: The source of our problem is that we have been unfaithful to God and fallen in love with the world (vv. 4-6). The Old Testament has numerous references describing the people of God as a wife who has been unfaithful to her husband: Isaiah 57:3-9; Jeremiah 3:6-10; Ezekiel 16:32-42; Hosea 3:1. The church is the bride of Christ, and he has a right to expect our love. Falling in love with the world is a betrayal of our wedding vows and expresses a hatred of God. Our desires and envy make us enemies of God and all that he stands for.

God gave us free will; then we used our freedom to choose against God and became attracted to evil. But God gives grace, freely extending his grace and forgiveness to the humble (James 4:6; Proverbs 3:34).

BIBLE TRUTH 3

We must submit to God. JAMES 4:7-10

■ **Many of us have trouble apologizing. Why do you think it is hard to say "I'm sorry" sometimes?**

INSIDE STORY: This points the way to the solution for our predicament—humble submission to God (vv. 7-10). To *submit* is a military term, meaning to put ourselves under authority and to be prepared to obey commands. When we submit to God, we stop resisting his will for our lives. Instead, we *resist* Satan (another military term), and he will run away from us! By contrast, when we approach God, he will come to us (v. 8).

But how dare we come near to God? We are unclean—we can't meet God like this! (Isaiah 6:5). Only "he who has clean hands and a pure heart" can come into God's presence (Psalm 24:4). That's why we cleanse our hands and hearts by confessing our sins (1 John 1:9). We repent of pretending to love God while loving the fallen world at the same time.

When we come to grips with the enormity of our sin we will "grieve, mourn and wail" (James 4:9). When we do mourn about our sinfulness, Jesus promises us that we will be comforted (Matthew 5:4). Since it's hard to repent while we're still laughing and having a good old time, the first step is to turn our laughter and joy into mourning and gloom. Then the Lord can step in and provide true joy. Finally, we *humble* ourselves, recognizing our low estate, before the Lord (James 4:10). We sorrowfully admit our unworthiness and gladly acknowledge his majesty. Surprisingly, when we do this, God does not gloat. ("I knew you'd come crawling back!") Instead, just as Jesus promised (Luke 18:14), God lifts up the humble and rewards us with Heaven.

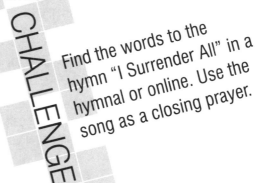

CHALLENGE

Find the words to the hymn "I Surrender All" in a hymnal or online. Use the song as a closing prayer.

Copyright © 2009 Standard Publishing. All rights reserved. Permission to photocopy for ministry purposes only—not for resale.

Power Up

Nature's Fury

Florida experienced a record-breaking year in 2004. But it wasn't a good kind of record. In that year, Florida was the first state to be hit by four hurricanes in one season since 1886, when Texas suffered that many. After the havoc, how did residents begin to rebuild?

First, people needed their electrical power restored. More than 1.7 million Florida homes and businesses lost power because of Hurricane Jeanne. The Florida Power & Light Co. (FPL) was receiving fifty thousand calls an hour from customers who needed assistance after that late September storm. The damage was less than Hurricane Frances a month before, but the manpower available was also much less. FPL called in eight thousand outside contractors to help restore the 2.8 million people without power from Frances. But only 2,800 workers were available to help with the Jeanne restoration. And only 1,500 of those workers were trained to fix electrical transformers and downed power lines. So FPL called in help from as far away as California and Canada.

Then, people tried to solve the sewage problems. About a week after Hurricane Ivan crashed through Pensacola in mid-September, sewer stations remained broken and neighborhoods began filling with muck. They had to fix this problem quickly since it causes major health concerns. Some people tried alternative methods to using the sewage system. One family showered in their swimsuits under a hose in the yard. But others continued to proceed as normal.

"I have learned that you cannot tell people to stop flushing, even after you explain it comes out onto their own street," said sewage technician Kennie Lyons.

Another step in the recovery process was helping farmers get grants or no-interest loans to begin again. The storms destroyed roughly $2.1 billion in Florida's cash crops. The U.S. Department of Agriculture supplied $500 million in loans and grants for citrus growers.

Finally, many people wanted to rebuild another important aspect of Florida—its reputation. Florida tourism is a $51 billion a year industry. Miami Beach Mayor David Dermer tried to get the word out that his city and southeast Florida hadn't been damaged by the storms.

Andy Newman, with Florida Key Tourism Development Council, agreed, saying, "We have to get the message out that the entire state of Florida has not been devastated."

QUESTIONS
TO CONSIDER:

■ Name the types of power you find in this article. When we hear the word "power," we may think of electricity, but think about the power of teamwork as people came in to help Florida rebuild, the power of money that farmers needed to start over, the power of reputation as people decided whether or not to spend their vacations in Florida, and the power of images as people around the world were able to see the devastation in Florida. Which power do you think is the most important and why?

■ The residents of Florida also relied on the power of prayer, whether they realized it or not. People who lived there or across the country prayed to God on their behalf. Today we're going to read in James about three ways that prayer is powerful.

INSTANT**STUDY 40** ■ NEW**TESTAMENT**

Copyright © 2009 Standard Publishing. All rights reserved. Permission to photocopy for ministry purposes only—not for resale.

BIBLE**TRUTH** 1

Prayer is a source of emotional strength. JAMES 5:13

■ **When are you most likely to pray—when you are happy or sad? Why?**

INSIDE STORY: A person who has emotional strength is well equipped to face a crisis. The prophet Nahum proclaimed that God is "a refuge in times of trouble" (Nahum 1:7). In prayer we allow God to be our fortress (Psalm 9:9; 37:39), giving us the strength, wisdom, and support we need to make it through anything.

But note that the Bible instructs us to also pray when we are happy (James 5:13; Psalm 59:16). Bipolar disorder is a brain disorder involving extreme highs and lows in mood. A bipolar person can quickly move from a state of great happiness to feelings of extreme sorrow. While the causes and treatment of this dysfunction are complex, James's prescription is helpful. Prayer is equally valuable when we are on emotional mountaintops or in the deepest of emotional valleys.

BIBLE**TRUTH** 2

Prayer is a source of physical healing. JAMES 5:14, 15

■ **What are some differences between praying to God for healing and reciting a magical incantation for healing?**

INSIDE STORY: Much has been made lately in the popular press about scientific studies regarding the power of prayer to increase the success of recuperation from illness and surgery. ABCNews.com labeled one story, "Scientists Suggest Recovery May Be the Hand of God at Work." Cited were studies of AIDS patients, heart attack victims, and others who had a better-than-chance recovery rate when prayed for by church groups and others. Though it is nice that secular studies seem to indicate prayer is valid, Christians have always known this. James made it clear that a church is to unite in prayer for sick members (James

5:14). We need to be able to bring our needs to a concerned group of believers who care and will pray. Anointing with oil is also mentioned (v. 14). In Bible times oil was commonly used as a medicine. It is also used in Scripture as a symbol for the Holy Spirit. Both prayer and conventional medical treatment work together to bring physical healing.

BIBLE**TRUTH** 3

Prayer is a source of spiritual renewal. JAMES 5:16

■ **Think of a time when you felt that God was far away from you. Why do you think you felt that way?**

INSIDE STORY: Above and beyond physical healing is spiritual renewal. Sin does serious damage to our spiritual health. God's medicine for sin is confession, prayer, and forgiveness. There are times when it is necessary to confess not only to God, but also to one another. If we've sinned against someone, we must clear it up. If we are struggling with a pattern of sin, we need to seek help. If we are suffering from guilt for a confessed sin, others can step in with loving reassurance. By confessing to each other, the healing of broken relationships and broken hearts takes place.

The final thought of James in this passage should stand as an encouragement to us. God has declared us righteous—in right standing—before him because of our faith in Jesus Christ (Romans 3:22). In response, we are to "make every effort to be found spotless, blameless and at peace with him" (2 Peter 3:14). Those who do will enjoy powerful and effective prayer lives.

CHALLENGE

Bring a small flashlight and turn it on. Then remove the batteries. Point out that without the power of prayer, we are much like the flashlight in that condition. Pass the flashlight from person to person with each giving a sentence prayer asking for God's power to work in a specific way in his or her life.

Copyright © 2009 Standard Publishing. All rights reserved. Permission to photocopy for ministry purposes only—not for resale.

SCRIPTURE INDEX

OLD TESTAMENT

NEW TESTAMENT

SCRIPTURE TOPIC INDEX

STORY TOPIC INDEX

DISCUSS

>IT<

Get teens talking and involved in Bible lessons with thought-provoking discussion starters! *Discuss It* uses a variety of methods to engage students in meaningful conversation including:

- Case studies
- Role plays
- Quizzes
- Challenges
- Deep questions

Photocopy these grayscale talk sheets as a starting place to design lessons, devotions, youth talks, events, or to enhance existing lesson materials. This is a fully-indexed, convenient, affordable, and easy-to-use resource that youth leaders will want to keep at their fingertips.

Each talk sheet also appears as a full-color, projectable image on the enclosed CD!

Discuss It–50 Role Plays and Case Studies to Get Teens Talking
Price: $10.99
Item #: 40406

Discuss It–50 Quizzes, Challenges, and Deep Questions to Get Teens Talking
Price: $10.99
Item #: 40407

To order, call 1–800–543–1353 or visit www.standardpub.com.

Standard®
PUBLISHING
Bringing The Word to Life